Book 2

ACTIVE
Skills for Communication

Chuck Sandy • Curtis Kelly

Series Consultant:
Neil J. Anderson

HEINLE
CENGAGE Learning

Australia • Brazil • Japan • Korea • Mexico • Singapore • Spain • United Kingdom • United States

HEINLE
CENGAGE Learning

**ACTIVE Skills for Communication,
Student Book 2**
Sandy / Kelly / Anderson

Publisher: Andrew Robinson

Editorial Manager: Sean Bermingham

Senior Development Editor: Ian Purdon

Associate Development Editor:
Lauren Rodan

Director of Global Marketing: Ian Martin

Content Project Manager: Tan Jin Hock

Senior Print Buyer: Mary Beth Hennebury

Editorial and Production Project Management:
Content*Ed Publishing Solutions, LLC

Illustrator: Raketshop Design Studio

Compositor: Chrome Media Group / C. Hanzie

Cover Designer: Chrome Media Group /
M. Chong / C. Hanzie

Cover Images: All photos from Shutterstock,
except bottom (Photos.com)

Photo Credits

Photos.com: pages 13 (top and center), 15, 25,
37, 39 (all except top and bottom right), 44
(all except top left and center), 55 (center and
bottom left), 59, 69 (all except right), 71, 73
(top and bottom left), 76 (top), 77, 83, 89, 100;
iStockphoto: pages 13 (bottom), 16, 23, 26, 29
(all except bottom right), 31, 33, 39 (top and
bottom right), 40 (bottom row), 41, 43 (left and
center), 55 (top and bottom right), 57 (all except
top center), 60, 63 (bottom), 65, 69 (right),
99; Index Open: pages 29 (bottom right), 73
(center and bottom right); Shutterstock: pages
40 (top left), 43 (right), 47, 51, 57 (top center),
63 (top), 67, 75, 76 (all except top), 81, 85, 93
(right), 95, 101, 103, 104, 107, 109, 111, 115; Photo
Objects: pages 40 (top right), 44 (top left and
center); Chrome PhotoDisc: page 49; The Kobal
Collection: page 93 (left)

Student Book ISBN-13: 978-1-4130-2032-8
Student Book ISBN-10: 1-4130-2032-1
Book + Student Audio CD ISBN-13: 978-1-4240-0909-1
Book + Student Audio CD ISBN-10: 1-4240-0909-X

Heinle
20 Channel Center Street
Boston, Massachusetts 02210
USA

Cengage Learning is a leading provider of customized learning solutions with office
locations around the globe, including Singapore, the United Kingdom, Australia, Mexico,
Brazil, and Japan. Locate our local office at:
international.cengage.com/region

Cengage Learning products are represented in Canada by Nelson Education, Ltd.

Visit Heinle online at **elt.heinle.com**
Visit our corporate website at **www.cengage.com**

Printed in Canada
2 3 4 5 6 7 8 9 10   13 12 11 10

DEDICATION AND ACKNOWLEDGMENTS

This book is dedicated to our families who have patiently endured our long periods of writing, and who have helped so much along the way with comments, suggestions, love, and support. We'd also like to dedicate this book to our students over the years for bearing with us as we tried out early versions of the activities that became ACTIVE Skills for Communication. By teaching us what learning is, they helped shape the ideas from which this course has arisen. Thanks go, too, to our editors at Cengage Learning, who have supported this project from the time it was first proposed several years ago. Their belief in our approach and vision for the course has been an enormous blessing. Particular thanks go to Chris sol Cruz, who first embraced the idea of ACTIVE Skills for Communication, Sean Bermingham and Guy De Villiers, who helped shape our approach, and Ian Purdon, who tirelessly worked with us through each and every page of the many versions of each unit. We could not have done it without you.

Our hope is that teachers around the world can use this series as a way to engage and motivate their learners, and that their students will be as successful in doing the activities and as enriched by them as our students have been.

We appreciate enormously the input we received from students and teachers in Korea, Thailand, Taiwan, Japan, Brazil, and the United States, including Oral Communication students at Osaka Gakuin and Heian Jogakuin Universities, and Oral Strategies students at Chubu University. We would especially like to thank Dr. Yoshiyasu Shirai, Anne Shirai, Daryl Aragaki, and Rex Tanimoto at Osaka Gakuin University.

Chuck Sandy & Curtis Kelly

Reviewers

Daryl Aragaki, Osaka Gakuin University; **Mayumi Asaba**, Osaka Gakuin University; **Rima Bahous**, Lebanese American University; **Phillip Barkman**, Asia University; **Edmar da Silva Falcão**, CEI—Centro De Ensino De Idioma; **Muriel Fujii**, Osaka Gakuin University; **John Gebhardt**, Ritsumeikan University; **Chris Hammond**, Kyoto Gakuen University; **Ann-Marie Hadzima**, National Taiwan University; **Brian Heldenbrand**, Jeonju University; **Caroline C. Hwang**, National Taipei University of Technology; **Mitsuyo Ito**, Osaka Gakuin University; **Hiroshi Izumi**, Tomigaoka Super English High School; **Kristin L. Johannsen**, ELT specialist, the United States; **Leina Jucá**, MAI English; **Steve Jugovich**, Seikei Sports University; **Yuco Kikuchi**, English Pier School owner; **Michelle Misook Kim**, Kyung Hee University; **Kevin Knight**, Kanda University of International Studies; **Sumie Kudo**, Osaka Gakuin; **Hae Chin Moon**, Korea University; **Adam Murray**, Tokyo Denki University; **Heidi Nachi**, Ritsumeikan University; **Miho Omori**, Keirinkan; **Bill Pellowe**, Kinki University; **Nigel Randell**, Ryukoku University; **Alex Rath**, Shih Hsin University; **Gregg Schroeder**, ELT specialist, Hong Kong; **Pornpimol Senawong**, Silpakorn University; **Jeffrey Shaffer**, Shimane University; **Kyoko Shirakata**, ELT specialist; **Masahiro Shirai**, Doshisha Girls' Junior and Senior High Schools; **Thang Siew Ming**, Universiti Kebangsaan Malaysia; **Stephen Slater**, ELT specialist; **Wang Songmei**, Beijing Institute of Education; **Scott Smith**, Kansai Gaidai University; **Joe Spear**, Hanbat National University; **Rex Tanimoto**, Osaka Gakuin University; **Ellen Tanoura**, Osaka Gakuin University; **Dave Tonetti**, Kyung Hee University; **Matthew Walsh**, Momoyama Gakuin High School and Ikeda High School; **James Webb**, Kansai Gaidai University; **Nancy Yu**, ELT specialist

SCOPE AND SEQUENCE

Unit	Challenge	Skills	Fluency	Language
1. Class Facebook *Page 13*	Designing a personal emblem for someone	Greeting people; Sharing personal information	Back-channelling to show you are listening	**Interrogatives** Where did you go to high school?, Have you ever traveled abroad? **Verb phrases** used to, want to, be going to, would like to **Infinitives** work, travel, improve, etc. **Personal information** school, interests, future plans, etc.
2. Personal Motto *Page 21*	Making and explaining a personal motto	Expressing opinions and explaining what something means	Asking for clarification	**State of being verbs** I think (that) . . ., I believe (that) . . . **Adjectives** open-minded, creative, smart, etc. **Prepositions** during, away, at, etc.
3. Tall Tales *Page 29*	Telling stories in a truth/lie game	Telling a story	Referring back to something the speaker said	**Past progressive tense & past simple tense** I was riding the bus yesterday, when I found a phone. **Sequencing expressions** after a while, just then, as soon as, etc. **Storytelling expressions** You won't believe this., Well, . . ., Anyway, . . . **Adjectives** scary, surprising, irritating, etc.
Project 1. Digital Story *Page 37*		**Recycling themes and language from Unit 3** Making a story and presenting it in an electronic format		
4. Keepsakes *Page 39*	Presenting a personal item and explaining why it is special	Describing the past	Shadowing the speaker's words	**Keepsake items** a good luck charm, a childhood toy, a family heirloom, etc. **Time expressions** ago, since, for, etc. **Past simple tense** I got my first guitar one year ago. **Present perfect tense** I have had this guitar for one year / since last year. **Present perfect continuous tense** I have been taking guitar lessons for one year / since Christmas.
5. Team Spirit *Page 47*	Discussing and presenting ways to develop good relationships	Making suggestions to improve the class	Disagreeing with someone else's ideas	**Plural/singular nouns** information, ideas, advice, etc. **Infinitives** *like to* + infinitive **Discussion expressions** Why don't we . . ., How about . . ., What do you think?, etc.
6. Hot Spots *Page 55*	Making an advertisement and recommending a business	Describing likes and dislikes	Responding to suggestions	**Locations** fitness center, coffee shop, shopping mall, etc. **Adjectives** friendly, cozy, delicious, etc. **Gerunds & infinitives** I enjoy/dislike/don't mind trying new restaurants. I like/love/hate going to the mall. I like/love/hate to go to the mall. **Activities** go on a date, buy a new laptop, get some fresh air, etc.
Project 2. Radio Ad *Page 63*		**Recycling themes and language from Unit 6** Advertising an upcoming event		

Unit	Challenge	Skills	Fluency	Language
7. Class Cookbook *Page 65*	Making and explaining an interesting food recipe	Giving instructions	Slowing down the conversation	**Cooking-related vocabulary** verbs, cooking utensils, taste/flavor adjectives **Imperatives** Chop an onion and some garlic into small pieces. **Sequencing expressions** First, Next, While, etc.
8. Business Venture *Page 73*	Planning and presenting a new business idea	Explaining key features of a business	Hesitating	**Businesses** shop, restaurant, delivery service, etc. **Definite or indefinite articles** *the*, *a*, or *an* **Business vocabulary** name, products, location, etc.
9. Job Interview *Page 81*	Role-playing interviewing someone and being interviewed	Describing work experience and abilities	"Mirroring" the speaker	**Verb phrases** work alone, work with other people, work at home, etc. *Some* or *any* Do you have any computer experience? **Modals and related expressions** should, ought, be able to, have to, need to **Job-related vocabulary** professions, skills, qualifications, work experience
Project 3. Job Fair *Page 89*		**Recycling themes and language from Unit 9** Researching careers and presenting ideas		
10. TV Preview *Page 91*	Performing a trailer for a TV show or movie	Describing likes and dislikes, and what something is about	Speaking dramatically	**TV show & movie vocabulary** soap opera, quiz show, action movie, etc. **Relative clauses** *who* or *that* *24* is a TV series about a guy who tries to stop terrorists. **Adjectives** nervous, romantic, strict, etc.
11. Public Opinion *Page 99*	Telling a story about a problem and asking classmates what they would do	Presenting a story and predicting reaction.	Introducing opinions	**Hypothetical situations** What would you do if you were Ally? If I were Ally, / If I were in that situation, / If that happened to me, I'd . . . **Reporting results** Everyone / Most people / A few people / One person / No one said that . . .
12. Mini Debate *Page 107*	Planning a debate issue and debating in small groups	Expressing opinions, supporting arguments, agreeing, and disagreeing	Illustrating your point (giving examples)	*Nobody, somebody, everybody* **Position statements** I personally feel that . . ., I strongly disagree that . . ., etc. **Debate issues** Health, society, environment, education
Project 4. Future Plans *Page 115*		**Evaluating progress and successes from Student Book 2** Self-evaluation and presentation		
Audio Scripts and "Spoken English"	*Page 117*			

5

To learners:

Welcome to *Active Skills for Communication*. Here are some suggestions to help you get as much as possible from this course.

▸ First, be active. Make using and learning English your personal goal. Be active in learning English by being active in using it.

▸ Second, don't be afraid to make mistakes. Each mistake is a step toward learning.

▸ Third, be aware of how communication involves critical thinking and decision making. This thinking is an important part of learning.

▸ Fourth, develop learning strategies. Decide what you need to learn. Then, find the ways to learn that best fit your style.

▸ Fifth, learn how the different parts of a unit work, so that you can get the most out of them.

▸ In short, be positive toward communicating in English. There are many new experiences waiting for you in the pages that follow.

Chuck Sandy & Curtis Kelly

To teachers:

What are the basic characteristics of this course?

First, it is goal-oriented. Each unit builds toward a final speaking activity, such as an interview, a presentation, a game, a role-play, or a discussion. These *Challenge* activities are more than straightforward language exercises—they foster meaningful interaction between students and are based on real situations language learners face both inside and outside of the classroom.

Second, it is strategy-oriented. Interacting in English requires a greater repertoire of skills than just being able to produce the right grammar and vocabulary. It requires learners to identify goals, choose strategies, speak expressively, and respond appropriately. Learners are encouraged to think critically about the language they are learning, thereby helping them integrate communication strategies into real interactions.

Finally, it makes learners active. Personalized speaking activities throughout the course give learners ownership of their interactions and their learning. When students use English to relate real experiences, frame real opinions, and respond genuinely to others, English becomes more than something to study. It becomes something to broaden their perspectives.

ARE YOU AN *ACTIVE* COMMUNICATOR?

Before you use this book to develop your communication skills, think about your speaking and listening habits, and your strengths and weaknesses when communicating in English. Check [✔] the statements that are true for you.

1. I look for chances to use English.
   ☐ Start of course   ☐ End of course

2. I sometimes speak English with people who speak my first language.
   ☐ Start of course   ☐ End of course

3. I enjoy communicating in English with English speakers.
   ☐ Start of course   ☐ End of course

4. I think communicating in English is fun.
   ☐ Start of course   ☐ End of course

5. I tell myself "speaking English is easy."
   ☐ Start of course   ☐ End of course

6. I don't mind making pronunciation, vocabulary, or grammar mistakes.
   ☐ Start of course   ☐ End of course

7. If the listener does not understand something, I try to say it in a different way.
   ☐ Start of course   ☐ End of course

8. I listen to how other people say things in English, such as in movies or music.
   ☐ Start of course   ☐ End of course

9. When I listen, I try to get the message rather than try to understand every word.
   ☐ Start of course   ☐ End of course

10. If I can't understand what someone is saying very well, I guess.
    ☐ Start of course   ☐ End of course

11. I'm a good listener—I listen carefully to what other people are saying.
    ☐ Start of course   ☐ End of course

12. I don't answer questions with just one word, such as "yes" or "no." I say more.
    ☐ Start of course   ☐ End of course

13. I try to think in English before speaking, rather than translate from my language.
    ☐ Start of course   ☐ End of course

14. I participate in class, talking as much as I can.
    ☐ Start of course   ☐ End of course

15. I sometimes review what we study in class at home.
    ☐ Start of course   ☐ End of course

16. I plan to travel to an English-speaking country if I can.
    ☐ Start of course   ☐ End of course

At the end of the course, answer the quiz again to see if you have become a more fluent, active communicator.

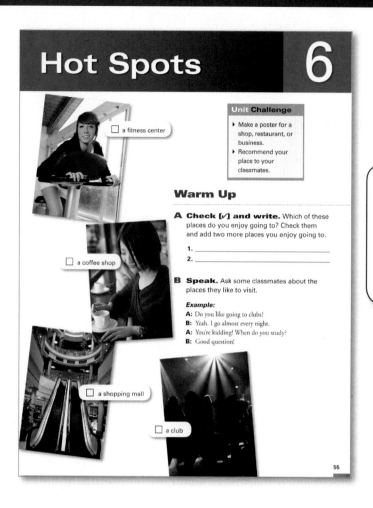

1. Each unit begins with the *Warm Up*. This page gets you thinking about the unit topic, and will help you talk about your life and your experiences. For example, there are units on your personal values and on your career goals.

2. The *Challenge Preview* demonstrates what you are going to do in the *Challenge*—that's the major speaking activity at the end of the unit. This page presents the language you will need to do the *Challenge*. Listen to some students doing the *Challenge*, and do the activities to help you prepare.

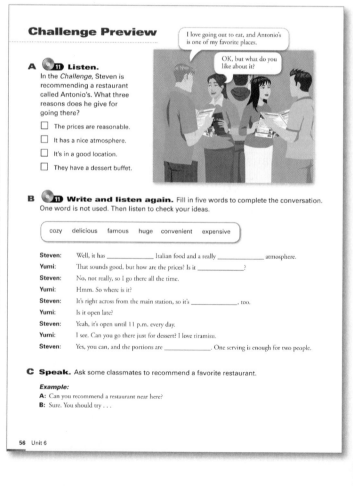

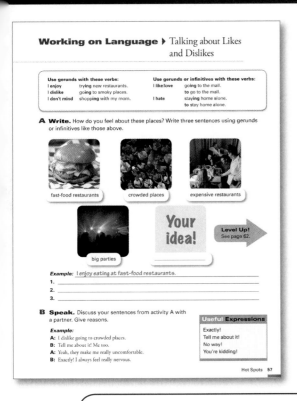

Working on Language ▶ Talking about Likes and Dislikes

Use gerunds with these verbs:		Use gerunds or infinitives with these verbs:	
I enjoy	trying new restaurants.	I like/love	going to the mall.
I dislike	going to smoky places.		to go to the mall.
I don't mind	shopping with my mom.	I hate	staying home alone.
			to stay home alone.

A Write. How do you feel about these places? Write three sentences using gerunds or infinitives like those above.

fast-food restaurants   crowded places   expensive restaurants

Your idea!

Level Up! See page 62.

big parties

Example: I enjoy eating at fast-food restaurants.

1. _____
2. _____
3. _____

B Speak. Discuss your sentences from activity A with a partner. Give reasons.

Example:
A: I dislike going to crowded places.
B: Tell me about it! Me too.
A: Yeah, they make me really uncomfortable.
B: Exactly! I always feel really nervous.

Useful Expressions
Exactly!
Tell me about it!
No way!
You're kidding!

Hot Spots **57**

---

3. *Working on Language* teaches you what to say in the *Challenge*. Simple charts and activities help you structure your ideas, and allow you to talk about yourself with your classmates. *Useful Expressions* also help you interact with your classmates more freely.

---

4. *Communicate* extends what you have learned in the unit so far. It also gives you more opportunities to talk with your classmates about the unit topic.

Note to teacher: The end of this page is a good place to stop if you are teaching the unit in two lessons.

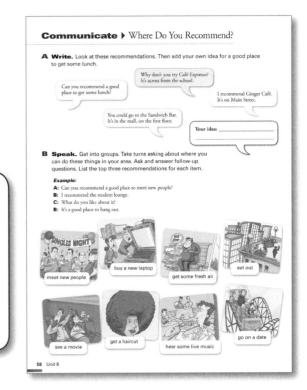

Communicate ▶ Where Do You Recommend?

A Write. Look at these recommendations. Then add your own idea for a good place to get some lunch.

Can you recommend a good place to get some lunch?

Why don't you try Café Espresso? It's across from the school.

I recommend Ginger Café. It's on Main Street.

You could go to the Sandwich Bar. It's in the mall, on the first floor.

Your idea: _____

B Speak. Get into groups. Take turns asking about where you can do these things in your area. Ask and answer follow-up questions. List the top three recommendations for each item.

Example:
A: Can you recommend a good place to meet new people?
B: I recommend the student lounge.
C: What do you like about it?
B: It's a good place to hang out.

meet new people   buy a new laptop   get some fresh air   eat out

see a movie   get a haircut   hear some live music   go on a date

58 Unit 6

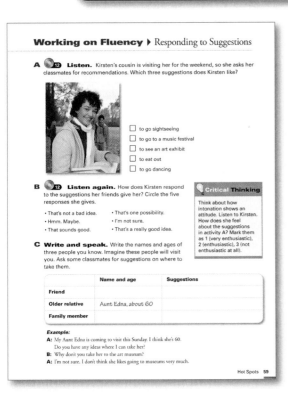

Working on Fluency ▶ Responding to Suggestions

A 🔊 12 **Listen.** Kirsten's cousin is visiting her for the weekend, so she asks her classmates for recommendations. Which three suggestions does Kirsten like?

- ☐ to go sightseeing
- ☐ to go to a music festival
- ☐ to see an art exhibit
- ☐ to eat out
- ☐ to go dancing

B 🔊 12 **Listen again.** How does Kirsten respond to the suggestions her friends give her? Circle the five responses she gives.

- • That's not a bad idea.
- • Hmm. Maybe.
- • That sounds good.
- • That's one possibility.
- • I'm not sure.
- • That's a really good idea.

Critical Thinking
Think about how intonation shows an attitude. Listen to Kirsten. How does she feel about the suggestions in activity A? Mark them as 1 (very enthusiastic), 2 (enthusiastic), 3 (not enthusiastic at all).

C Write and speak. Write the names and ages of three people you know. Imagine these people will visit you. Ask some classmates for suggestions on where to take them.

	Name and age	Suggestions
Friend		
Older relative	Aunt Edna, about 60	
Family member		

Example:
A: My Aunt Edna is coming to visit this Sunday. I think she's 60. Do you have any ideas where I can take her?
B: Why don't you take her to the art museum?
A: I'm not sure. I don't think she likes going to museums very much.

Hot Spots **59**

---

5. *Working on Fluency* helps you speak more fluently and do the *Challenge* more successfully.

Listen to the conversations on the CD and then engage in deeper conversations with your classmates.

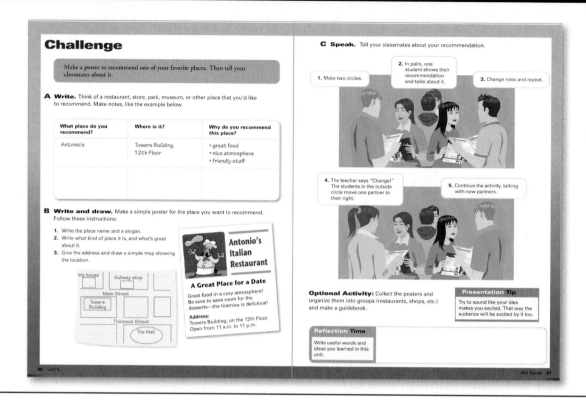

6. The *Challenge* is the major speaking activity at the end of the unit. Each *Challenge* is based on a situation you're likely to face, or a skill you're likely to need, to communicate in English—both inside and outside of the classroom. The *Challenges* include games, interviews, and role-plays.

Some *Challenges* will ask you to make a presentation. Read the presentation tips and practice them to become a confident and effective presenter.

When doing the *Challenge*, don't worry about using perfect English. Instead, concentrate on getting the *Challenge* done using only English. The *Challenge* gets you to use everything you learned to really *communicate* with your classmates.

The reflection time helps you organize and record language that's important to you.

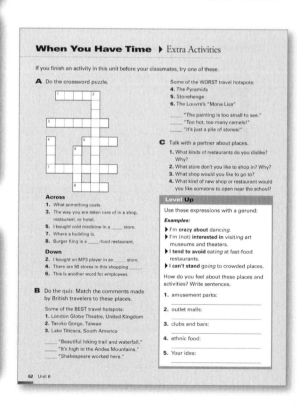

7. Try the fun *When You Have Time* activities when you finish an activity before your classmates. Some can be done alone, and others are speaking activities to be done in pairs.

The *Level Up* material gets you to think about what you have learned, and develop your language skills.

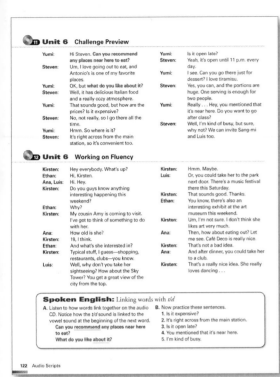

🔊11 Unit 6 Challenge Preview

Yumi: Hi Steven. **Can you recommend any places near here to eat?**

Steven: Um, I love going out to eat, and Antonio's is one of my favorite places.

Yumi: OK, but **what do you like about it?**

Steven: Well, it has delicious Italian food and a really cozy atmosphere.

Yumi: That sounds good, but how are the prices? Is it expensive?

Steven: No, not really, so I go there all the time.

Yumi: Hmm. So where is it?

Steven: It's right across from the main station, so it's convenient too.

Yumi: Is it open late?

Steven: Yeah, it's open until 11 p.m. every day.

Yumi: I see. Can you go there just for dessert? I love tiramisu.

Steven: Yes, you can, and the portions are huge. One serving is enough for two people.

Yumi: Really . . . Hey, you mentioned that it's near here. Do you want to go after class?

Steven: Well, I'm kind of busy, but sure, why not? We can invite Sang-mi and Luis too.

🔊12 Unit 6 Working on Fluency

Kirsten: Hey everybody. What's up?

Ethan: Hi, Kirsten.

Ana, Luis: Hi. Hey.

Kirsten: Do you guys know anything interesting happening this weekend?

Ethan: Why?

Kirsten: My cousin Amy is coming to visit. I've got to think of something to do with her.

Ana: How old is she?

Kirsten: 19, I think.

Ethan: And what's she interested in?

Kirsten: Typical stuff, I guess—shopping, restaurants, clubs—you know.

Luis: Well, why don't you take her sightseeing? How about the Sky Tower? You get a great view of the city from the top.

Kirsten: Hmm. Maybe.

Luis: Or, you could take her to the park next door. There's a music festival there this Saturday.

Kirsten: That sounds good. Thanks.

Ethan: You know, there's also an interesting exhibit at the art museum this weekend.

Kirsten: Um, I'm not sure. I don't think she likes art very much.

Ana: Then, how about eating out? Let me see. Café Deco is really nice.

Kirsten: That's not a bad idea.

Ana: And after dinner, you could take her to a club.

Kirsten: That's a really nice idea. She really loves dancing . . .

Spoken English: Linking words with *t/d*

A. Listen to how words link together on the audio CD. Notice how the *t/d* sound is linked to the vowel sound at the beginning of the next word.
Can you recommend any places near here to eat?
What do you like about it?

B. Now practice these sentences.
1. Is it expensive?
2. It's right across from the main station.
3. Is it open late?
4. You mentioned that it's near here.
5. I'm kind of busy.

Communicate More

At the back of the book, the *Spoken English* material (pages 117–128) gets you thinking about how native speakers of American English really talk. When speaking, native speakers of American English often change the way they pronounce certain words and phrases.

PROJECT **1**

Digital Story

Make a story with pictures and words using Powerpoint, or another kind of presentation software, and present it to your classmates.

A Discuss. These students are talking about the digital stories they plan to make. Which idea do you like the best?

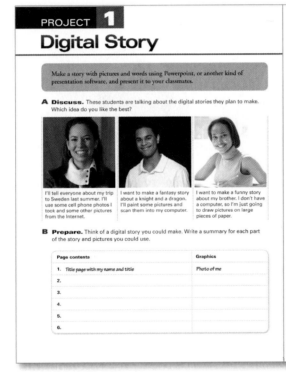

I'll tell everyone about my trip to Sweden last summer. I'll use some cell phone photos I took and some other pictures from the Internet.

I want to make a fantasy story about a knight and a dragon. I'll paint some pictures and scan them into my computer.

I want to make a funny story about my brother. I don't have a computer, so I'm just going to draw pictures on large pieces of paper.

B Prepare. Think of a digital story you could make. Write a summary for each part of the story and pictures you could use.

Page contents	Graphics
1. Title page with my name and title	Photo of me
2.	
3.	
4.	
5.	
6.	

C Create. Make a digital story like the example below.* If you don't have a computer, draw pictures and write the story on large pieces of paper. Then practice reading your story.

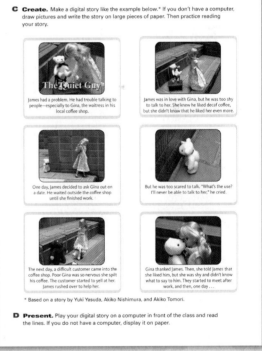

The Quiet Guy
James had a problem. He had trouble talking to people—especially to Gina, the waitress in his local coffee shop.

James was in love with Gina, but he was too shy to talk to her. She knew he liked decaf coffee, but she didn't know that he liked her even more.

One day, James decided to ask Gina out on a date. He waited outside the coffee shop until she finished work.

But he was too scared to talk. "What's the use? I'll never be able to talk to her," he cried.

The next day, a difficult customer came into the coffee shop. Poor Gina was so nervous she spilt his coffee. The customer started to yell at her. James rushed over to help her.

Gina thanked James. Then, she told James that she liked him, but she was shy and didn't know what to say to him. They started to meet after work, and then, one day . . .

* Based on a story by Yuki Yasuda, Akiko Nishimura, and Akiko Tomori.

D Present. Play your digital story on a computer in front of the class and read the lines. If you do not have a computer, display it on paper.

Projects

The *Projects* take learning beyond the classroom. You'll do research and prepare outside of class, and then present your project to your classmates. Each project will give you the chance to express yourself. There are four in this student book: a digital story, a radio advertisement, a job fair, and a self-evaluation.

CLASSROOM LANGUAGE

Language you will hear in the class:

Open your books to Unit 1.

Listen to the conversation.

Compare answers with a partner.

Find a partner.

Let's do part A.

Look at the *Warm-up* page.

Make groups of four.

Work by yourself.

Language you will want to use in class:

Could you say that again, please?

What does _____ mean?

Did you say (page 12)?

How do you say _____ in English?

Luis

Kirsten

Could you explain this activity again?

We've finished the activity.

Steven

Sang-mi

What should we do next?

How do you spell that?

Language you will use to work with a partner or in groups:

I'll go first.

What do you think?

It's your turn.

How about you?

Yumi

Ethan

That's a good idea!

Ana

Thanks for telling me.

Unit Challenge

▶ Interview a classmate.
▶ Design a personal emblem for him/her.

Warm Up

Speak. To get to know your classmates better, introduce yourself and ask questions.

Hi, Hannah. It's good to see you.

It's good to see you, too, Darren.

What's your schedule like this semester, Sarah?

Pretty good. I only have five classes.

Are you taking any interesting classes?

Yes. "Introduction to Film." It sounds fun.

Challenge Preview

A  **Listen.**

Some students are doing the *Challenge* at the end of this unit. Ana designed an emblem for Luis. What does each picture in Luis' emblem represent—the past, the present, or the future?

1. book _____

2. soccer shoes _____

3. airplane _____

Hi everyone, I'm Ana. I designed this emblem for Luis.

B  **Write and listen again.** Fill in five words to complete the conversation. One word is not used. Then listen to check your ideas.

> work   have   travel   improve   get   play

Ana: When Luis was in high school, soccer was a big part of his life, so I drew a pair of soccer shoes. Luis used to _____ soccer on the high school team. They won the national championship.

Steven: Really? That's great.

Ana: Anyway, this book represents Luis' life now. He wants to _____ his grades, so he is going to _____ harder this year. This picture of a book represents that.

Steven: Uh-huh.

Ana: This airplane represents the future. Luis said he'd like to _____ around the world someday. He also wants to _____ a job in a foreign country.

C **Speak.** What do you think these symbols represent? Talk with a partner about the meaning of each symbol.

Example:

A: What do you think the first symbol represents?

B: I think it represents family.

A: Maybe—but it could represent friends or friendship.

1.

2.

3.

4.

Working on Language ▶ Asking Questions

A Write. Complete the questions and answers using the words below.

What were	What's
Did you	Why did
Who's your	What kind of
~~Where did you~~	Have you ever

~~a school near Taipei.~~	play a lot of tennis.
Justin Timberlake.	music and fashion.
kind of shy.	my own business.
Australia last year.	a good reputation.

1. ___Where did you___ go to high school?   I went to ___a school near Taipei.___

2. _____ you like in high school?   I was _____

3. _____ play any sports in junior high?   I used to _____

4. _____ you decide to study at this school?   It has _____

5. _____ traveled abroad?   Yes, I went to _____

6. _____ things you are interested in?   I'm really into _____

7. _____ favorite singer these days?   I really like _____

8. _____ one of your goals for the future?   I'd like to start _____

B Speak. Ask a partner the questions above. Your partner will answer with real information.

Level Up!
See page 20.

Example:
A: Where did you go to high school?
B: I went to a school near Taipei. How about you?
A: Me too. My school was just outside the city.
B: Oh really? What was it called?
A: Maybe you know it. It was called . . .

Useful Expressions

That's nice.
How interesting!
Me too. / Me neither.
Not me.

Communicate ▶ Who's the Same?

A Write. Imagine you're talking to Hiroshi, Liz, or David. What questions would you like to ask them? Share your ideas with your classmates.

TV is a big part of my life. I turn the TV on as soon as I wake up in the morning. My TV is always on. —David

Example: _Which TV shows do you like to watch?_

1. _____

_____

Music is really important to me. I used to play in a band, and now I work part-time as a DJ at a club. —Hiroshi

2. _____

_____

3. _____

_____

My family gets together every weekend for dinner. We're all very close. That's me on the left. —Liz

4. _____

_____

5. _____

_____

B Speak and write. Ask your classmates questions about their interests and relationships. Write one way you're the same as each person and one way you're different. Don't write the same thing twice.

Example:

A: Do you watch a lot of TV, Miguel?
B: Yeah. I turn on the TV as soon as I wake up in the morning.
A: Me too. I love game shows.
B: Not me. I prefer talk shows and soap operas.

Name	We both . . .	However . . .
Miguel	like TV.	he prefers talk shows and soap operas.

Working on Fluency ▶ Backchanneling

A 💿 2 **Listen.** Ana asks her classmates three different questions. What question is each person answering? Number the questions.

_____ What would you like to do in the future?

_____ What's your hometown like?

_____ What were you like in high school?

B **Listen again.** Listen to the conversations again. Check [✔] the six things Ana says to show she is listening.

☐ Hmm.   ☐ OK.   ☐ Right.   ☐ Mm-hmm.

☐ That's nice.   ☐ I see.   ☐ Really?   ☐ Uh-huh.

C **Speak.** Ask a partner one of the questions below. Try to show you are listening by using the follow-up questions and expressions in activity B.

▸ What's one of your goals for this year?

▸ What's your family like?

▸ What was high school or junior high like for you?

▸ What's the most interesting place you have ever been to?

> 💡 **Critical Thinking**
>
> Think about other ways to show you are listening and are interested in the conversation. List at least three ideas and use them when you are doing activity C.

Example:

A: What's one of your goals for this year?

B: I'd like to visit Australia.

A: Mm-hmm. Where in Australia?

B: I'd like to go to Sydney.

A: Uh-huh. Why Sydney?

B: I'd like to see the Opera House.

Challenge

Interview a partner. Find out interesting things about your partner's past, present, and future. Then design a personal emblem for your partner.

A Speak. Interview a partner and fill in the personal information on the Class Facebook worksheet on page 19.

B Write and speak. Write questions to ask about your partner's past, present, and future. Then interview your partner and take notes.

Past experiences:

1. _____

2. _____

Present life:

1. _____

2. _____

Future goals:

1. _____

2. _____

C Create. Make an emblem for your partner.

D Speak. Tell your classmates about your partner. Then, work together to combine the worksheets to make a class facebook.

Class Facebook

Personal Information

1. Name: _____
2. Birthday: _____
3. Hometown: _____
4. Contact Information:

_____

Present

Past

Future

Insert a photo or draw a picture here.

More Information:

Reflection Time

Write useful words and ideas you learned in this unit.

When You Have Time ▶ Extra Activities

If you finish an activity in this unit before your classmates, try one of these.

A Do the celebrity crossword puzzle.

```
          ¹J
          A
       ²P[ ][ ][ ]    ³[ ]
   ⁴[ ]  A
⁵[ ][ ][ ][ ][ ]N   ⁶[ ]
   ⁷[ ][ ][ ][ ]    [ ]
      [ ]            [ ]
      ⁸[ ][ ][ ][ ][ ][ ]
```

Across

2. Morgan Freeman's first acting jobs were in _____ in Broadway theaters.

5. Vivian Hsu is from Taichung, in _____.

7. Jennifer Lopez is a dancer, _____, and actor.

8. Avril Lavigne is from Ontario, _____.

Down

1. Actor Bae Yong Joon is more popular in _____ than in Korea.

3. When singer Bon Jovi was young, he often skipped _____.

4. Sean Connery was the _____ James Bond in earlier 007 movies.

6. Bill Gates' dream is to stop AIDS in _____.

B Do the classmates quiz. Who do you think:

◇ is good at English?   _____

◇ likes making friends?   _____

◇ likes shopping?   _____

◇ likes spicy food?   _____

◇ travels a lot?   _____

C Talk with a partner about your class goals.

1. Do you know anyone in this class? How well?

2. Who in this class would you like to get to know better?

3. What kinds of things would you like to do in this class?

4. What language skill would you like to improve most?

Level Up

You can also make questions more polite by using "Do you mind if I ask . . ."

Examples:

Where did you go to school? ▶
Do you mind if I ask where you went to school?

Are you from around here? ▶
Do you mind if I ask if you're from around here?

Rewrite these questions using "Do you mind if I ask" to make them more polite. Then ask and answer with a partner.

1. Where did you grow up?
_____

2. What kind of music do you like?
_____

3. What's your favorite TV show?
_____

4. Are you married?
_____

5. What other classes are you taking?
_____

Personal Motto

Never say never.

Kindness costs nothing.

Practice makes perfect.

Don't worry. Be happy.

Warm Up

A **Check [✓] and write.** A motto is a short phrase or sentence that expresses a rule for sensible behavior. Choose two mottos you like. Then write one more motto you know.

Your idea: _____

_____

B **Speak.** Tell your partner about the mottos you chose.

Example:

A: I really like "Never say never."

B: Oh really? What do you like about it?

A: I think it's important to be positive. That's what this motto is all about.

Challenge Preview

A 🔘3 **Listen.**

In the *Challenge*, Yumi is explaining her motto to Ethan. Which idea do you think Yumi had before creating her own motto?

My motto is "Friends first." I think it's important to be considerate and caring. My friends are important to me.

☐ I'm a pretty easygoing person.

☐ Friends are more important than other people.

☐ I should meet my friends every day.

B 🔘3 **Write and listen again.** Fill in five words to complete the conversation. One word is not used. Then listen to check your ideas.

> in   during   at   inside   in   away

Yumi: Let me explain. Last year, I moved _____ from home and entered college.

Ethan: Uh-huh.

Yumi: There were so many new things _____ my life—a new school, new classmates—so I started to forget my old high school friends.

Ethan: Mm-hmm. So what happened?

Yumi: We stopped calling each other. Then, when I went home _____ the vacation, I called my old friends but they were all "too busy" to meet me. I was really upset.

Ethan: Right. So what did you do?

Yumi: Well, I realized how important those old friends were. They were angry _____ me because I didn't stay _____ touch. So, I called them and apologized. Now, we're all friends again, and we keep in touch.

C **Speak.** What are three important things in your life? Tell a partner.

Example:
A: Three important things in my life are my weekends, music, and my band.
B: Your weekends?
A: I'm really busy most of the time, so it's the only time I get to relax.

Working on Language ▶ Expressing Opinions

Personality traits	More information
I think (that) I'm a pretty friendly and outgoing person.	I enjoy talking with people.
I believe (that) it's important to be optimistic and positive.	I try to look on the bright side of things.

A Check [✓] and match.
Check the statements that are true for you. Then draw a line from each statement to the correct personality trait.

1. ☐ I enjoy helping others.
2. ☐ I always try to tell the truth.
3. ☐ I like talking with people.
4. ☐ Nothing gives me stress.
5. ☐ I make people laugh.
6. ☐ I work hard to achieve my goals.
7. ☐ I try to look on the bright side of life.
8. ☐ No one can tell me how to live my life.

a. friendly and outgoing
b. optimistic and positive
c. hardworking and ambitious
d. laid-back and relaxed
e. kind and generous
f. strong and independent
g. humorous and entertaining
h. honest and sincere

B Write. How would you describe your personality? Write sentences using the ideas above or others of your own.

Example: I think I'm a really neat and organized person. I like making lists of things I have to do.

1. _____

2. _____

C Speak. Describe other students in your class.
Use the ideas above to help you.

Example:
A: Bill, you seem like a friendly and outgoing person.
B: Thanks, but why do you think that?
A: You said "hello" to a few people when you came in the room.
B: That's nice of you to say.

> **Useful Expressions**
>
> Thanks for noticing.
> That's nice of you to say.
> I don't think so, but thanks.
> That's interesting. My friends say the same thing.

Communicate ▶ What's Important to You?

A Write. Choose three topics you would like to talk about with a partner. Make a list for each topic.

Three important people in your life: 1. _____ 2. _____ 3. _____	**Three things you cannot live without:** 1. _____ 2. _____ 3. _____	**Three positive qualities you wish you had:** 1. _____ 2. _____ 3. _____
Three people you admire: 1. _____ 2. _____ 3. _____	**Three personality traits you do not like in other people:** 1. _____ 2. _____ 3. _____	**Three places you want to visit someday:** 1. _____ 2. _____ 3. _____
Three important things your parents taught you: 1. _____ 2. _____ 3. _____	**Three qualities you think a romantic partner should have:** 1. _____ 2. _____ 3. _____	**Three things you would like to change about yourself:** 1. _____ 2. _____ 3. _____

B Speak. Tell a partner about what you wrote. Your partner will ask you follow-up questions.

Example:

A: One of the most important people in my life is my brother, Leo.

B: Why is he so important to you?

A: Because he's really kind and generous.

B: What do you mean? Can you give me an example?

A: When I have a problem, he listens and gives me advice.

Sample follow-up questions:

What do you mean?	Can you give me an example?	What is that?
Why is that?	Can you tell me more?	Why is that important to you?

Working on Fluency ▶ Asking for Clarification

A 🔘4 **Listen.** A reporter is interviewing a DVD rental company president, Mr. Coleman. Which questions does the reporter ask? Check [✔] them.

☐ What does that mean?

☐ Do you mean you know what movies I like?

☐ What do you mean by "sure"?

☐ Where can I find out more about them?

☐ Why do you think so?

☐ Can you give me an example?

☐ Can you tell me what "DVD" means?

☐ May I ask what's special about your movies?

B Write. Complete the sentences about yourself using adjectives. Then complete the chart, and explain what you mean.

Example: I used to be a ____clumsy____ child.

1. I used to be a(n) _____ child.

2. I grew up in a(n) _____ town with a(n) _____ family.

3. In the future, I would like to be (more / ~er) _____ than I am now.

Word	Meaning
clumsy	I broke things all the time.

C Speak. Read your sentences from activity B to a partner. Your partner will ask you to explain what you mean, using the questions in activity A.

Example:

A: I used to be a pretty clumsy child.

B: What do you mean by "clumsy"?

A: Well, I broke things all the time.

B: Can you give me an example?

A: Well, one time I smashed a window with a soccer ball.

💡 Critical Thinking

Think about the different ways "What do you mean?" is used after these statements. What intonation should you use?

1. I'm sorry. I can't go out with you tonight.
2. My motto is "Friends first."

Write a short conversation using "What do you mean?" Then practice it with a partner.

Challenge

Make a personal motto for yourself, and tell others what it means.

A **Write.** What are some of your most important rules, values, or goals? Write three sentences about yourself, like these examples.

I believe that it's important to put my friends first.

I want to be more optimistic and stop worrying about things.

I'm really adventurous, so I want to travel around the world someday.

1. _____

_____

2. _____

_____

3. _____

_____

B **Write.** Choose one of your sentences from activity A. Write the number of your sentence below and shorten it to make a motto.

Sentence	▶	Motto
Putting my friends first.	▶	Friends first.
Don't worry about things.	▶	No worries.
Live an adventurous life.	▶	See the world!
Your sentence number: _____	▶	_____

Level Up!
See page 28.

C Create. Write your name and personal motto on the front of a card. Then write notes on the back of the card about what your motto means.

Friends first.

—Yumi

What does your motto mean?

How does it help your life?

- **Friends are very important to me.**
- **We should always stay in touch.**
- **I can make new friends but mustn't forget my old friends.**
- **My motto helps me remember these things.**

Why is your motto important to you?

D Speak. Walk around the classroom, holding your card so that others can read your motto. Look at other students' mottos and ask them questions.

Example:
A: Hi Yumi, what's your motto?
B: It's "Friends first."
A: What does it mean?
B: It means . . .

Reflection Time

Write useful words and ideas you learned in this unit.

When You Have Time ▶ Extra Activities

If you finish an activity in this unit before your classmates, try one of these.

A What company slogans do these businesses have? Match each business to its slogan.

1. McDonald's (a fast-food restaurant)
2. LG (an electronics company)
3. Nike (a sportswear maker)
4. Vodafone (a cell phone company)
5. Tower Records (a CD store)
6. Apple (a computer company)

_____ JUST DO IT ™

_____ Think Different ™

_____ NO MUSIC, NO LIFE ™

_____ How are you?

_____ i'm lovin' it ™

_____ Life's Good ™

B How many of these English proverbs do you know? Match to make sentences.

1. A bird in the hand
2. Actions speak louder
3. Rome wasn't built
4. Love
5. When the cat is away,

a. in a day.
b. is blind.
c. than words.
d. the mice will play.
e. is worth two in the bush.

C Talk with a partner about learning English.

1. What English word or expression do you like?
2. Are there any English words or expressions you don't like?
3. What are good ways to learn new words?
4. What English dialect or accent would you like to learn? Why?

Level Up

A simile is a figure of speech that compares two unlike things using the words *like* or *as . . . as*. Similes help us understand something in a new way.

Examples:
Life is like a highway.
My friends are as necessary as air.

Complete the sentences with your own ideas. Then compare with a partner and explain what they mean.

1. Life is like _____
   _____

2. These days, I'm as _____
   as _____

3. Love is like _____
   _____

4. My friends are as _____
   as _____

5. _____
   _____

taking a trip

Unit Challenge

▸ Tell short stories.
▸ Take part in a story-telling game.

Warm Up

Speak. Tell a partner about these experiences. Your partner will ask you follow-up questions.

Example:

A: I took a short trip last summer.
B: Really? Where did you go?
A: My friends and I spent a week in London.
B: That sounds fun.

going to a concert

losing something important

seeing something unusual

Challenge Preview

A 〔CD 5〕 **Listen.**

In the *Challenge*, Sang-mi is telling a story to her classmates. What happened to her in the subway?

> Listen to this. I had a really embarrassing experience recently.

☐ She got on the wrong train by accident.

☐ She met a very old friend by accident.

☐ She thought someone was talking to her and he wasn't.

B 〔CD 5〕 **Write and listen again.** Fill in four expressions to complete the conversation. One expression is not used. Then listen to check your ideas.

> after a while   just then   last month   as soon as   next time

Sang-mi: I was taking the subway _____ when this guy sat down next to me. _____ he sat down, he said, "Hey, it's Kevin. How are you doing?"

Ethan: Did you know him?

Sang-mi: No, I didn't, but he was kind of cute, so I said, "I'm pretty good, thanks. How about you, Kevin?"

Ethan: And what did he say?

Sang-mi: Nothing—he didn't say anything, but _____ he asked, "What have you been doing recently?" Well, I thought that was a strange question, but I said, "Nothing much. How about you?"

Ethan: And?

Sang-mi: Well, he didn't answer, so I stood up and started to walk away. _____, I heard him say "Let's have dinner." So, I turned to the guy and said, "Sorry. I don't think I know you." He just looked at me and said, "Do you mind? I'm on the phone."

C **Speak.** Do you think this is a true story? Why or why not?

Example:
A: I think it really happened.
B: Really? I'm not sure. There is something strange about it.
A: What do you mean?
B: Well, the guy is in the subway, right? So, . . .

Working on Language ▶ Telling a Story

Start with the place and time
You won't believe this.   I was riding the bus yesterday, when I found a phone.

Explain what happened
Well, . . . /   It started to ring, so I picked it up. Then a man's voice
What happened next was, . . .   said, "You're late again! You're fired." I said, "Sorry,
                                           this isn't my phone," and hung up.

End with the outcome
Anyway, . . .   I felt really sorry for the phone's real owner.

A Number and speak. Sort the stories into the correct order. Then practice telling them to a partner. Use the storytelling expressions above.

Story 1

_____ I ran to get the lifeguard, and I told him about the woman.

_____ I thought it was a woman in trouble.

_____ I felt really embarrassed.

_____ I was walking on the beach last summer when I saw something in the water.

_____ The lifeguard said, "That's not a woman. That's a piece of wood."

Story 2

_____ The woman was waving at someone behind me.

_____ It looked like my mom, so I waved back.

_____ Then, I realized it wasn't my mom.

_____ I felt so stupid.

_____ I was shopping downtown last week when I saw someone waving.

B Speak. Get into groups. Choose one of these sentences and start a story. Each person adds a sentence to the story. Try to keep the story going as long as possible.

▶ I was jogging in the park yesterday, when I saw something really surprising.
▶ About a month ago, I decided to change my life.
▶ Once, I met a very strange person.
▶ Last week, I went to school, but no one was there.

Listen to this. I was jogging in the park yesterday when I saw something really surprising.

It was a clown.

What happened next was, he said, "Are you here for the circus too?" . . .

Communicate ▸ What's Your Story?

A Write. You are going to tell some stories. Choose two of the situations below and make notes to help you remember your stories.

What/When/Where	Start the story	End the story
• something funny • last week • in a movie theater	• woman behind me • talking on the phone	• I complained • It was my mom!

B Speak. Tell your stories to other students.

Example: You won't believe this. I was watching a movie last week at a theater, and there was a woman sitting behind me. She was so noisy. She was talking and talking on her cell phone . . .

Useful Expressions

You're kidding!
Then what happened?
That's embarrassing!

Working on Fluency ▶ Referring Back

A  **Listen.** A woman in an office is asking a work colleague what happened to her missing apple. What does the woman say to check the man's story? Complete the sentences.

> You told me that . . .   You said that . . .
> You mentioned that . . .   You claimed that . . .

1. _____ you made a cup of coffee.

2. _____ you got milk from the fridge.

3. _____ the fruit wasn't in the fridge.

4. _____ the apple was gone.

B Write. Read the story below. Then write three questions to check details.

> Last week, I was jogging in the park when I found a wallet. There was a lot of money in it. When I got home, I called the wallet's owner. That evening, we met at a coffee shop and he said I could keep some of the money.

Example: You said that you were in a park.
               Which park did you go to?

1. _____

2. _____

3. _____

C Speak. Tell a partner about something you recently did. When you finish, your partner will ask you questions like those above.

Example:

A: Last Saturday, I met a friend downtown. We went shopping together and bought some clothes.

B: You said that you went shopping with a friend. Who went with you?

A: Oh, I went with Jerry.

💡 Critical Thinking

Think about how the verbs "claim" and "mention" change the tone of a statement.

For example:

1. You claimed you were home last night (*but no one answered when I called*).

2. You mentioned that you were home last night (*so I wondered what you watched on TV*).

How would you start the sentence ". . . you went out last night (*but I saw you online*)." to check the story?

Challenge

Get into groups of three and tell stories in front of the class: two stories are true, and one is made up. The class will guess which story is not true.

A **Discuss and write.** Get into groups of three. Two students think of true stories, and the other student creates a made-up story. Choose a situation from the *Communicate* page, or make up one of your own. Develop your stories by filling in the chart.

You won't believe this. Something really embarrassing happened to me last month . . .

Start with a place and time:	Explain what happened:	End with an outcome:

B **Prepare.** Write out your stories on pieces of paper. Add details to make them more believable.

Good: I went out to dinner.

Better: I went out to Jeannette's Grill for a celebration dinner.

C Speak. Practice telling your stories to people in your group. Your group members will ask you questions like this:

> **Example:** You claimed you were on the subway last month.
> What day was it?

D Present. In groups, tell your three stories to your classmates. The class will vote which student is telling the made-up story. Give one point for each correct guess.

Presentation Tip

If you have a conversation in a story, use different voices for different people, such as a high voice for a child.

Reflection Time

Write useful words and ideas you learned in this unit.

When You Have Time ▶ Extra Activities

If you finish an activity in this unit before your classmates, try one of these.

A Find the missing adjectives in the word search.

```
D S E F R A S I A D
E E S E R D A U E I
S Y S C A R Y Y Y F
S N N I Y O O M Y R
A E Y T R N E P R D
R M Y N N P M Y I C
R Y N A N A R Y R A
A E M M Y U C U R O
B N N O B R F R S U
M S N R Y M D Y A O
E N U E U O R N E C
```

1. Your boyfriend/girlfriend took you to a French restaurant. It was so _____.

2. You fell off the stage at your graduation ceremony. You were really _____.

3. However, when another person fell off the stage, it was really _____.

4. You were so _____ when someone took two seats on the crowded subway.

5. A bird flew in your bedroom window. You were really _____.

6. On a cold, dark night walking home alone, you heard footsteps behind you. It was very _____.

B Do the celebrity quiz. True or false?

1. _____ The American comedian Jim Carrey dropped out of school in the ninth grade.

2. _____ The Hong Kong actor Jackie Chan has a hole in his head from a filming accident.

3. _____ The American actor Brad Pitt asked his wife to marry him on the day he met her for the first time.

4. _____ The Japanese singer Ayumi Hamasaki is ambidextrous (can write with both right and left hands).

5. _____ The American actor Tom Cruise has a hearing problem.

C Talk with a partner about stories.

1. What was your favorite book when you were growing up?

2. What video have you watched again and again? Why?

3. Do you enjoy listening to gossip?

4. What are some traditional folk stories you would/wouldn't want to tell a child?

Level Up

Stories are often told in the "graphic present" tense—as if they're happening now. It makes them sound more exciting.

Example: So, I'm sitting in the park when this guy says "hello" and asks me how my family is. I don't recognize him at all, so I ask him who he is. He looks at me and says, "I'm your cousin."

Rewrite the following story by changing the verbs to graphic present tense. Then practice telling the story to a partner.

So, I was walking through campus when this girl told me she liked the song I was singing. I didn't even realize I was singing, so I just smiled and walked away.

_____

_____

_____

PROJECT 1

Digital Story

Make a story with pictures and words using PowerPoint, or another kind of presentation software, and present it to your classmates.

A Discuss. These students are talking about the digital stories they plan to make. Which idea do you like the best?

I'll tell everyone about my trip to Sweden last summer. I'll use some cell phone photos I took and some other pictures from the Internet.

I want to make a fantasy story about a knight and a dragon. I'll paint some pictures and scan them into my computer.

I want to make a funny story about my brother. I don't have a computer, so I'm just going to draw pictures on large pieces of paper.

B Prepare. Think of a digital story you could make. Write a summary for each part of the story and pictures you could use.

Page contents	Graphics
1. Title page with my name and title	Photo of me
2.	
3.	
4.	
5.	
6.	

C Create. Make a digital story like the example below.* If you don't have a computer, draw pictures and write the story on large pieces of paper. Then practice reading your story.

James had a problem. He had trouble talking to people—especially to Gina, the waitress in his local coffee shop.

James was in love with Gina, but he was too shy to talk to her. She knew he liked decaf coffee, but she didn't know that he liked her even more.

One day, James decided to ask Gina out on a date. He waited outside the coffee shop until she finished work.

But he was too scared to talk. "What's the use? I'll never be able to talk to her," he cried.

The next day, a difficult customer came into the coffee shop. Poor Gina was so nervous she spilt his coffee. The customer started to yell at her. James rushed over to help her.

Gina thanked James. Then, she told James that she liked him, but she was shy and didn't know what to say to him. They started to meet after work, and then, one day . . .

* Based on a story by Yuki Yasuda, Akiko Nishimura, and Akiko Tomori.

D Present. Play your digital story on a computer in front of the class and read the lines. If you do not have a computer, display it on paper.

Keepsakes

4

☐ a good luck charm

☐ a childhood toy

Unit Challenge

▸ Show something you own to your classmates.
▸ Explain what the item is and why it is important to you.

Warm Up

A Check [✓] and write. Do you have any of these things? Check the things you own. Then add one more keepsake.

Your idea: _____

_____

B Speak. Discuss your keepsakes with a partner.

Example:

A: Do you have any old letters?
B: Yes, I do. I have all the letters from my first boyfriend.
A: Really? I never keep old letters.

☐ a family heirloom

☐ an old souvenir

☐ old letters

Challenge Preview

What did you bring to class, Kirsten?

This necklace.

A 💿 **7 Listen.**

In the *Challenge*, Kirsten is telling Luis about one of her keepsakes. Why is it special for her?

☐ It was a gift from her mom.

☐ Her grandmother bought it for her.

☐ It reminds Kirsten of her grandmother.

B 💿 **7 Write and listen again.** Fill in five words to complete the conversation. One word is not used. Then listen to check your ideas.

> during   ago   since   when   for   until

Luis: May I ask why it's special for you?

Kirsten: My mom gave it to me _____ I graduated from high school.

Luis: So you got it a few years _____, right?

Kirsten: Yes, that's right. I've had it _____ three years.

Luis: It's nice. Do you wear it often?

Kirsten: Yeah, I've worn it every day _____ graduation.

Luis: It must be very special to you.

Kirsten: Yes, it's very special. If I have a daughter, I'll keep it _____ she graduates and then give it to her.

C Speak. Here are some other students' keepsakes. Why do you think they are special? Talk with a partner.

Example:

A: Why do you think this penny is special for Yumi?

B: Well, it's from the U.S. Maybe she took a trip to America.

1 Yumi

2 Ethan

3 Steven

4 Sang-mi

Working on Language ▶ Talking about the Past

<table>
<tr><td>What</td><td>When</td></tr>
<tr><td>I got my first guitar</td><td>one year ago.</td></tr>
<tr><td>I have had this guitar</td><td>for one year / since last year.</td></tr>
<tr><td>I have been taking guitar lessons</td><td>for one year / since Christmas.</td></tr>
</table>

A Read and circle. Choose the correct tense to make sentences about these keepsakes.

I play soccer every weekend. I *have been playing / played* for the local team *for / since* six years, and it *is / was* a big part of my life. I was named team captain *a year ago / since a year ago*, so when we won the championship, I *got / have got* the trophy. I *kept / have kept* this trophy in my room *for / since* then. Whenever I see it, I *remember / have been remembering* that day.

I *bought / have bought* this wallet with money I *earned / have been earning* at my first part-time job. I *feel / felt* so proud the day I bought it. I *carry / have been carrying* it every day *for / since* I was 17. That means *I've had / I've been having* it *for / since* almost five years. It looks kind of old now, but it *is / was* still one of my treasures.

B Write. Complete these sentences.

1. I (watch) _____ "New York Legal" on TV for two years and still love it.

2. I (take) _____ a trip to Hong Kong a month ago.

3. I (study) _____ English since I was in the fifth grade.

4. I (have) _____ this same hairstyle for ten years.

5. Your idea: _____.

C Speak. Tell a partner about your experiences and possessions. Your partner will ask follow-up questions to get more information.

Example:

A: I've been watching "American Idol" for about three years. It's the best show on TV.

B: Oh really? Who do you think will win this year?

A: I don't know. It's always a surprise.

Level Up! See page 46.

Communicate ▶ Special Memories

Speak. Play this game in groups.

How to play:

1. Use something in your bag as a marker.

2. Flip a coin and move your marker (heads = one space, tails = two spaces).

3. Ask a group member at least three questions about the square you land on (*What, When, Where*).

4. Continue until someone in your group reaches the goal.

Example:

A: Tell me about an award you got.

B: Well, I won a dance competition last month at school. There were about 100 contestants.

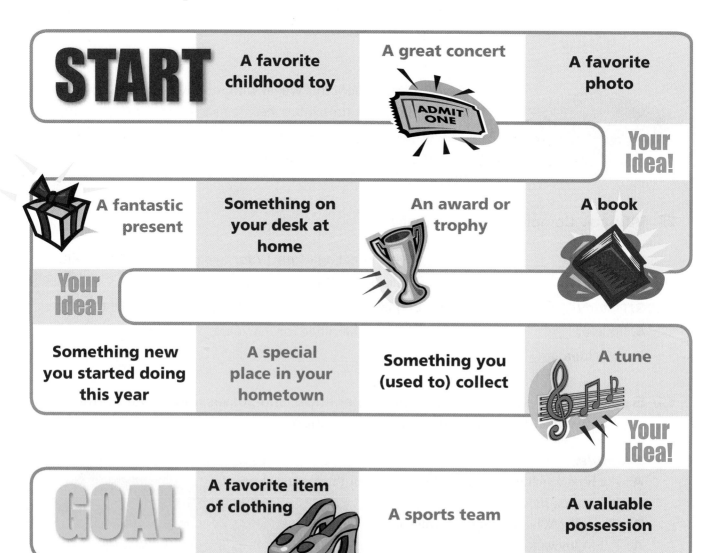

Working on Fluency ▶ Shadowing

A 💿 **8** **Listen.** Steven is telling Yumi about his keepsake—a book about cars. Which car does Steven describe? Check [✔] it.

B 💿 **8** **Listen again.** Sometimes Yumi shadows (repeats) Steven's words to show she is listening. Circle the three items she shadows.

- Italy
- a long time
- sports cars

- an old Fiat
- a library book
- four years ago

C **Speak.** Take turns telling a partner about one of these topics or another idea of your own. Your partner will shadow some of the things you say.

▶ your first pet
▶ your first trip abroad
▶ your first date
▶ your first bike

Example:
A: I have had a pet turtle since I was 14.
B: A pet turtle. What's its name?
A: I call it Hoover.
B: Hoover. That's interesting.

Critical Thinking

Think about how your tone of voice can show your feelings. Practice the example in activity C several times with a partner. Take turns being the speaker B, showing surprise, disbelief, boredom, and enthusiasm.

Challenge

Bring at least one keepsake to class to show your classmates. If you do not bring one, draw a picture of it instead.

A Write. Make notes about your keepsake, like the example below.

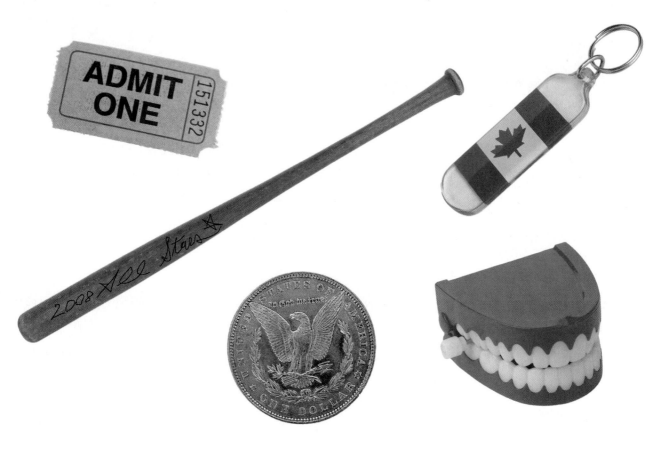

What is it?	Why is it special?	More information (who/when/where):
a signed baseball bat	reminds me of my friends and high school	We won the championship when I was 16 ...

B Speak and write. Tell a partner about your keepsake. Your partner will ask you as many questions as possible. Use your answers to make more notes in the chart in activity A.

Example:

A: When I was 16, my high school baseball team won the championship. This is the bat from that game.

B: What was the final score?

A: I forget, but I think it was 6 to 5.

B: Was this bat used in the game?

A: Yes, it was.

C Present. Show your keepsake to your classmates. The other students will listen and ask you questions.

Presentation Tip

Be a good listener. Help the speaker by shadowing, nodding your head, making eye contact, and asking questions.

Reflection Time

Write useful words and ideas you learned in this unit.

When You Have Time ▶ Extra Activities

If you finish an activity in this unit before your classmates, try one of these.

A What are these keepsakes? Find the missing words in the word search.

```
H  L  A  E  A  E  S  B  T  T
F  R  V  U  R  B  F  E  C  M
C  O  C  R  T  G  Y  O  O  S
L  L  U  L  O  B  I  A  O  S
L  C  G  R  A  N  D  M  A  B
N  F  S  B  S  A  O  S  E  I
L  R  E  S  H  E  L  L  S  E
T  E  K  C  I  T  R  B  E  N
O  B  U  M  L  D  T  O  U  S
S  E  T  Y  A  S  O  S  B  M
```

1. A good-luck charm, such as a _____-leaf clover.
2. A high school _____ with photos of classmates.
3. The first shoes worn by a _____.
4. Photos of a great grandpa and _____.
5. Paper money or _____ from a foreign country.
6. _____ collected on an ocean beach.
7. _____ letters from a romantic partner.
8. Half a _____ from a concert, play, or movie.

B Do the classmate quiz. Who do you think:

• is carrying a picture of a parent right now?

_____

• has a famous person's signature?

_____

• collects something unusual, such as bugs or stamps?

_____

• keeps photos of an ex-boyfriend/ex-girlfriend?

_____

• throws away old school papers and books?

_____

C Talk with a partner about keepsakes.

1. Do you have any pictures or other things on your desk or wall?
2. What homework papers do you keep?
3. Do you keep clothes you will never wear again?
4. Do you have a gift someone gave you that you don't use?

Level Up

The present perfect and present perfect continuous tenses are often used to ask questions.

Examples:
A: I've had this for a long time.
B: How long have you had it?
A: Since I was young.

A: I've been playing tennis for a long time.
B: How long have you been playing?
A: More than ten years.

Write follow-up questions to these statements using the present perfect tense or present perfect continuous tense. Then practice with a partner.

1. I've been living here for a long time.

_____

2. I've been studying English since I was little.

_____

3. I've had this flute since I was young.

_____

4. I've been taking yoga classes for a few years.

_____

5. I've wanted this trophy since junior high school.

_____

Team Spirit

Unit Challenge

▶ Discuss ways to develop good team relationships.
▶ Present your ideas to your classmates.

Warm Up

A Check [✓]. Which of these things would you like to do?

I'd like to:

☐ get to know my classmates better.

☐ learn how to study more effectively.

☐ get some extra help with my homework.

☐ spend time preparing for an exam.

☐ have a class party on the last day.

☐ get together with some classmates outside of school.

B Speak. Discuss your answers with a partner.

Example:
A: I'd really like to get to know my classmates better.
B: Yeah, me too. I don't even know everyone's name.

Challenge Preview

A 🔘9 **Listen.**

In the *Challenge*, a group of students are discussing a team spirit exercise. Which plan do they talk about?

☐ Getting Internet access for everyone in the class.

☐ Making a class website.

☐ Taking photos of everyone for a photo album.

> So, who would like to begin?

> I have an idea. Let's . . .

B 🔘9 **Write and listen again.** Are these count or noncount nouns? Write the letter *s* after the plural nouns when necesary to complete the conversation. Then listen to check your ideas.

Ana: We could use it to display information__.

Ethan: OK, but what kind of information__?

Ana: You know, about school news, homework assignment__, and other stuff__.

Ethan: Hmm. That sounds good.

Ana: Yes, and we could ask for advice__ and idea__ on how to study. As for me, I sometimes need help__.

Ethan: That's a really nice idea, Ana. Does anyone else have any suggestion__?

Sang-mi: You know, almost all of us have Internet access__, so we could put the bulletin board on a class website instead.

C Speak. Imagine your class is making a class website. What three things would you want it to have? Make a list and discuss with a partner.

Example: <u>We could include photos of everyone in the class.</u>

1. _____

2. _____

3. _____

Working on Language ▶ Making Suggestions to Improve Class

Introduce an idea	Make a suggestion	Ask for feedback
I have an idea.	Why don't we make a class website?	What do you think?
How about this?	We could make a class blog.	How does that sound?
Can I make a suggestion?	How about creating a photo gallery?	Would that work?

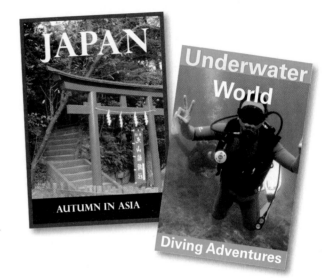

A Write. Suggest an idea to solve each of these common class problems.

Example: We could make the classroom more comfortable.

<u>I have an idea. Why don't we</u>
<u>decorate the room with</u>
<u>posters of interesting places.</u>
<u>What do you think?</u>

1. We want to improve our TOEIC® scores.

_____

2. We need some opportunities to speak English outside of class.

_____

3. We'd like to improve our reading ability.

_____

4. Students who miss class don't know what we studied.

_____

B Speak. Share your ideas in groups. Who has the best idea for each problem?

Example:
A: What could we do to make the classroom more comfortable?
B: I have an idea. How about decorating the room with posters of interesting places? Would that work?
A: That's a really nice idea. What kind of places?
B: Well, capital cities, for example.

Useful Expressions

That's a really nice idea.
That's one possibility.
I'm not sure.
Hmm. Maybe.

Communicate ▶ What Do You Think?

A Write. Brainstorm at least four more questions like these. Then choose one you'd like to use for a class survey.

- How could we learn each other's names? _____
- Where's a good place to go on a class trip? _____
- How can we communicate with each other after class? _____
- **1.** _____
- **2.** _____
- **3.** _____
- **4.** _____

B Speak. Ask six classmates the question you chose in activity A. Write down each person's best suggestion. Then tell your classmates about the most interesting suggestion you heard.

Example:

A: How could we learn each other's names? Any ideas?

B: Yeah. How about this? We could wear name tags. Would that work?

A: That's an interesting idea. Should we wear them the whole semester?

B: Maybe not. Let's just wear them for the first three weeks.

Level Up! See page 54.

Your question:	
Name:	**Suggestion:**
Jay	• wear name tags for the first three weeks

Working on Fluency ▶ Disagreeing

A 🔘 **10 Listen.** A group of students are discussing some ideas for class activities. How do they make sure that they work well together as a group? Check [✔] three answers.

☐ They choose a group leader.

☐ They vote on what they are going to do.

☐ They decide which person will take notes.

☐ They get several people to give ideas.

B 🔘 **10 Listen again.** Circle the phrases the speakers use when they disagree with another person's idea.

- That's an interesting idea, but . . .
- Actually, . . .
- I understand that, but . . .

- To tell you the truth, I'd rather . . .
- Yes, but . . .
- I have another suggestion.

C Speak. Work in groups. Discuss ways you could use $1,000 to improve your classroom. Use the phrases above when you want to disagree. Suggest as many different ideas as you can.

Example:

A: Well, what could we do with $1,000?

B: Can I make a suggestion? We could buy a DVD player for the classroom. How does that sound?

C: That's an interesting idea, but I'd rather start a class library . . .

💡 **Critical Thinking**

Think about things you could do or say in a group discussion to:

- make sure everyone has a turn to speak.
- make sure group members stay on task.
- get everyone in the group to speak English.

List one idea for each item.

Challenge

Discuss ways to improve the way your class works together. Then present your ideas to your classmates.

A **Speak and write.** Get into small groups, choose a group leader, and brainstorm ideas for a Team Spirit exercise. Write down and discuss everyone's ideas.

Example:

A: We could make T-shirts for everybody. How does that sound?

B: Yeah, and we could design a class logo to put on them.

C: Actually, it sounds a little complicated. How about something simple?

D: I was thinking about starting an English-only lunch table.

Team Spirit Ideas

- make T-shirts for everyone
- design a class logo
- start an English-only lunch table

B **Discuss.** As a group, choose the best idea. Discuss these points in as much detail as possible:

▸ What is your Team Spirit exercise exactly?

▸ How would it improve the way your class works together?

▸ How does it work?

▸ What's the best way to present your ideas to your classmates?

C **Present.** Present your Team Spirit exercise idea to your classmates, making sure that each group member has a role in the presentation.

> We have an idea for how to use English more outside of class, and we think it's pretty good. Monica will introduce the idea, Daniel will explain how it will help us, and Hannah will tell you how it works.

English-only Lunch

Make friends and practice English at the same time!

Where: School cafeteria, at the table by the window

When: Every Tuesday and Thursday

Contact person: Joe, tel. 555-1890

How's it going?

This is fun!

D **Speak.** Discuss the other groups' ideas and choose the best one. Do you have any suggestions to improve on that idea? Tell your classmates what you decide.

> We liked all the ideas, but we love the one about having an English-only lunch table. The idea is really good, but we'd like to make a suggestion. How about inviting some international students to join us? That would really . . .

Presentation Tip

For important or complicated information, say it slowly and clearly. Then repeat it. For example, "The lunch is only on Tuesdays and Thursdays. That's Tuesdays and Thursdays."

Reflection Time

Write useful words and ideas you learned in this unit.

When You Have Time ▶ Extra Activities

If you finish an activity in this unit before your classmates, try one of these.

A Find the missing words in the word search.

```
G  T  E  R  O  K  R  H  T  S
N  U  U  T  B  E  T  I  O  K
I  O  A  R  T  T  E  N  N  U
T  B  I  U  I  H  S  S  E  N
S  A  R  T  T  T  G  D  R  T
E  E  O  H  S  I  U  S  E  I
R  D  S  I  D  E  A  T  B  I
E  H  U  N  T  T  G  N  R  O
T  T  G  K  R  O  W  G  O  S
N  U  O  T  I  N  N  U  U  A
I  N  D  N  N  D  N  U  O  S
```

1. I have an _____.
2. How _____ this?
3. To tell you the _____, I'd rather . . .
4. Can I make a _____?
5. Would this _____?
6. That's an _____ idea.
7. What do you _____?
8. How does that _____?

B Do the activity quiz. Match the names of the festivals to their descriptions.

_____ Naked Festival, Japan
_____ Cockroach Racing, Australia
_____ Cheese Rolling Festival, United Kingdom
_____ Camel Wrestling, Turkey

1. People chase cheese down a hill, and often get hurt.
2. Two males fight until one runs away.
3. Insects race, and the fastest wins.
4. Men take their clothes off and run around the town.

C Talk with a partner about group work.

1. In this class, do you prefer working in groups, in pairs, or by yourself?
2. Do you like being the leader of the group?
3. How much do you speak when you work in a group?
4. What do you think is the best number of people to have in a discussion group?

Level Up

You can use "couldn't" and "shouldn't" to make polite suggestions when you feel very strongly about your ideas. "Couldn't" and "shouldn't" are more polite than "could" and "should."

Examples:
Could we make a class website? ▶
Couldn't we make a class website?

We should choose a class leader. ▶
Shouldn't we choose a class leader?

Change these sentences into polite questions. Then, compare with a partner.

1. We should make a list of everyone's email addresses.
   _____

2. We could get together after class.
   _____

3. Should we ask the teacher for some help?
   _____

4. We could invite some international students to join us.
   _____

5. Should we have this discussion in English?
   _____

Hot Spots

□ a fitness center

□ a coffee shop

□ a shopping mall

□ a club

Warm Up

A **Check [✓] and write.** Which of these places do you enjoy going to? Check them and add two more places you enjoy going to.

1. _____

2. _____

B **Speak.** Ask some classmates about the places they like to visit.

Example:

A: Do you like going to clubs?
B: Yeah. I go almost every night.
A: You're kidding! When do you study?
B: Good question!

Challenge Preview

A  🔊 11 Listen.

In the *Challenge*, Steven is recommending a restaurant called Antonio's. What three reasons does he give for going there?

- ☐ It has a nice atmosphere.
- ☐ The prices are reasonable.
- ☐ It's in a good location.
- ☐ They have a dessert buffet.

I love going out to eat, and Antonio's is one of my favorite places.

OK, but what do you like about it?

B 🔊 11 Write and listen again. Fill in five words to complete the conversation. One word is not used. Then listen to check your ideas.

> cozy   delicious   famous   huge   convenient   expensive

Steven: Well, it has _____ Italian food and a really _____ atmosphere.

Yumi: That sounds good, but how are the prices? Is it _____?

Steven: No, not really, so I go there all the time.

Yumi: Hmm. So where is it?

Steven: It's right across from the main station, so it's _____, too.

Yumi: Is it open late?

Steven: Yeah, it's open until 11 p.m. every day.

Yumi: I see. Can you go there just for dessert? I love tiramisu.

Steven: Yes, you can, and the portions are _____. One serving is enough for two people.

C Speak. Ask some classmates to recommend a favorite restaurant.

Example:

A: Can you recommend a restaurant near here?

B: Sure. You should try . . .

Working on Language ▶ Talking about Likes and Dislikes

Use gerunds with these verbs:		Use gerunds or infinitives with these verbs:	
I **enjoy**	try**ing** new restaurants.	I **like/love**	go**ing** to the mall.
I **dislike**	go**ing** to smoky places.		**to** go to the mall.
I **don't mind**	shopp**ing** with my mom.	I **hate**	stay**ing** home alone.
			to stay home alone.

A Write. How do you feel about these places? Write three sentences using gerunds or infinitives like those above.

fast-food restaurants

crowded places

expensive restaurants

big parties

Your idea!
_____

Level Up!
See page 62.

Example: I enjoy eating at fast-food restaurants.

1. _____

2. _____

3. _____

B Speak. Discuss your sentences from activity A with a partner. Give reasons.

Example:

A: I dislike going to crowded places.

B: Tell me about it! Me too.

A: Yeah, they make me really uncomfortable.

B: Exactly! I always feel really nervous.

Useful Expressions

Exactly!
Tell me about it!
No way!
You're kidding!

Communicate ▸ Where Do You Recommend?

A Write. Look at these recommendations. Then add your own idea for a good place to get some lunch.

> Can you recommend a good place to get some lunch?

> Why don't you try Café Espresso? It's across from the school.

> I recommend Ginger Café. It's on Main Street.

> You could go to the Sandwich Bar. It's in the mall, on the first floor.

> **Your idea:** _____
> _____
> _____

B Speak. Get into groups. Take turns asking about where you can do these things in your area. Ask and answer follow-up questions. List the top three recommendations for each item.

Example:

A: Can you recommend a good place to meet new people?
B: I recommend the student lounge.
C: What do you like about it?
B: It's a good place to hang out.

meet new people

buy a new laptop

get some fresh air

eat out

see a movie

get a haircut

hear some live music

go on a date

Working on Fluency ▶ Responding to Suggestions

A 🔘 **12** **Listen.** Kirsten's cousin is visiting her for the weekend, so she asks her classmates for recommendations. Which three suggestions does Kirsten like?

☐ to go sightseeing

☐ to go to a music festival

☐ to see an art exhibit

☐ to eat out

☐ to go dancing

B 🔘 **12** **Listen again.** How does Kirsten respond to the suggestions her friends give her? Circle the five responses she gives.

- • That's not a bad idea.
- • Hmm. Maybe.
- • That sounds good.
- • That's one possibility.
- • I'm not sure.
- • That's a really nice idea.

> 💡 **Critical Thinking**
>
> Think about how intonation shows an attitude. Listen to Kirsten. How does she feel about the suggestions in activity A? Mark them as 1 (enthusiastic), 2 (not enthusiastic).

C **Write and speak.** Write the names and ages of three people you know. Imagine these people will visit you. Ask some classmates for suggestions on where to take them.

	Name and age	Suggestions
Friend		
Older relative		
Family member		

Example:

A: My Aunt Edna is coming to visit this Sunday. I think she's 60.
    Do you have any ideas where I can take her?

B: Why don't you take her to the art museum?

A: I'm not sure. I don't think she likes going to museums very much.

Challenge

Make a poster to recommend one of your favorite places. Then tell your classmates about it.

A Write. Think of a restaurant, store, park, museum, or other place that you'd like to recommend. Make notes, like the example below.

What place do you recommend?	Where is it?	Why do you recommend this place?
Antonio's	Towers Building, 12th Floor	• great food • nice atmosphere • friendly staff

B Write and draw. Make a simple poster for the place you want to recommend. Follow these instructions:

1. Write the place name and a slogan.
2. Write what kind of place it is, and what's good about it.
3. Give the address and draw a simple map showing the location.

Antonio's Italian Restaurant

A Great Place for a Date

Great food in a cozy atmosphere! Be sure to save room for the desserts—the tiramisu is delicious!

Address:
Towers Building, on the 12th Floor.
Open from 11 a.m. to 11 p.m.

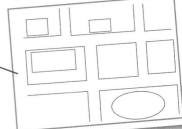

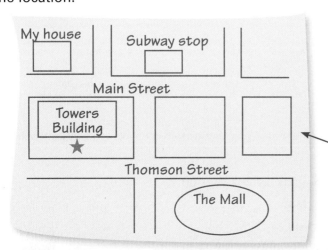

My house | Subway stop
Main Street
Towers Building ★
Thomson Street
The Mall

C Speak. Tell your classmates about your recommendation.

1. Make two circles. One circle inside the other.

2. In pairs, one student shows their poster and talks about it.

3. Change roles and repeat.

4. The teacher says "Change!" The students in the outside circle move one partner to their right.

5. Continue the activity, talking with new partners.

Optional Activity: Collect the posters, organize them into groups (restaurants, shops, etc.) and make a guidebook.

Presentation Tip

Try to sound like your idea makes you excited. That way the audience will be excited by it too.

Reflection Time

Write useful words and ideas you learned in this unit.

When You Have Time ▶ Extra Activities

If you finish an activity in this unit before your classmates, try one of these.

A Do the crossword puzzle.

```
    1 _ _ _ _ 2 _
              _
              _
  3 _ _ _ _ _ _ _
              _
  4 _     5 _ _ _ _
     _   6 _
     _     _
  7 _ _ _ _ _ _ _
         _
       8 _ _ _ _
```

Across

1. What something costs.
3. The way you are taken care of in a shop, restaurant, or hotel.
5. I bought cold medicine in a _____ store.
7. Where a building is.
8. Burger King is a _____-food restaurant.

Down

2. I bought an MP3 player in an _____ store.
4. There are 50 stores in this shopping _____.
6. This is another word for employees.

B Do the quiz. Match the comments made by British travelers to these places.

Some of the BEST travel hot spots:
1. London Globe Theatre, United Kingdom
2. Taroko Gorge, Taiwan
3. Lake Titicaca, South America

_____ "Beautiful hiking trail and waterfall."
_____ "It's high in the Andes Mountains."
_____ "Shakespeare worked here."

Some of the WORST travel hot spots:
4. The Pyramids
5. Stonehenge
6. The Louvre's "Mona Lisa"

_____ "The painting is too small to see."
_____ "Too hot, too many camels!"
_____ "It's just a pile of stones!"

C Talk with a partner about places.

1. What kinds of restaurants do you dislike? Why?
2. What store don't you like to shop in? Why?
3. What shop would you like to go to?
4. What kind of new shop or restaurant would you like someone to open near the school?

Level Up

Use these expressions with a gerund:

Examples:

▶ I'm **crazy about** danc*ing*.
▶ I'm (not) **interested in** visit*ing* art museums and theaters.
▶ I **tend to avoid** eat*ing* at fast-food restaurants.
▶ I **can't stand** go*ing* to crowded places.

How do you feel about these places and activities? Write sentences.

1. amusement parks:

   _____

2. outlet malls:

   _____

3. clubs and bars:

   _____

4. ethnic food:

   _____

5. Your idea:

   _____

Radio Ad

Prepare a radio advertisement to announce an upcoming event in your area and present it to others.

A Read and discuss. Read these announcements for upcoming events and the radio ads promoting them. Which event sounds most interesting to you?

Hi, and welcome to "Weekend Report." I'm DJ Jake. If you've always wanted to join a soccer team, here's your chance. The JB Regulars practice every Sunday at the school athletic field. New players are always welcome. Just meet on the field at noon and have some fun. Come out and enjoy yourself!

JB Regulars
Soccer practice every Sunday at noon, City University athletic field. New players welcome.

Hey everybody. I'm DJ Maxine with a hot tip for Friday night. The Living Room Café is hosting a World Party from 8 p.m. to midnight. It's just $20.00, and for that low price you get a buffet dinner, live music, and the chance to meet people from all over the world! Call 555-1212 to reserve. Why not give it a try? I'll be there!

World Party
Friday night. The Living Room Café. $20.00. Buffet dinner & live music. Call 555-1212 to reserve.

B Prepare. Check local newspapers and websites for upcoming events in your area. Then, choose one and take some notes.

Name of event: _____

Type of event: _____

Where/When: _____

Other information: _____

_____

C Create. Use the information you gathered to prepare a script for a radio ad. Use this outline or other ideas of your own.

Choose one of these opening lines to introduce yourself.

☐ This is DJ (name) _____ with a weekend tip for you.

☐ Hi, and welcome to "Weekend Report." I'm DJ (name) _____.

☐ Hey everybody. I'm DJ (name) _____ with a hot tip for (when) _____.

☐ Your idea: _____

_____

Explain the event.

_____

_____

_____

_____

End your radio ad.

☐ Be sure to check it out.

☐ Come out and enjoy yourself!

☐ Why not give it a try? I'll be there!

☐ Your idea: _____

_____

D Present. Take turns presenting your radio ad in groups or to the class. Which events sound the most interesting to you? Who sounds the most like a DJ?

Example:

"Hey everybody. I'm DJ Marco with a hot tip for Sunday afternoon. The White Street Café is hosting a Soccer Party from 2 p.m. to 8 p.m. . . ."

Class Cookbook

1. ☐ paella

2. ☐ udon noodles

3. ☐ guacamole and tortilla chips

Unit Challenge

▸ Make a recipe for a unique dish.
▸ Explain your recipe in front of the class.

Warm Up

A **Check [✓] and number.** Which dishes have you eaten? Check the pictures. Then match the dishes to the cuisines below.

| _1_ Spanish | _____ Korean | _____ Chinese |
| _____ Mexican | _____ Thai | _____ Japanese |

B **Speak.** Ask whether your partner has ever eaten these dishes.

Example:

A: Have you ever eaten tom yum soup?
B: No, I haven't. Is it good?
A: I like it. It's sweet and spicy.
B: Mmm. That sounds good.

Useful Words

spicy	salty	sweet
oily	tasty	plain
light	heavy	

4. ☐ dim sum

5. ☐ kimchee

6. ☐ tom yum soup

Challenge Preview

A  **13 Listen.**

In the *Challenge*, Ethan is explaining how to make his recipe. What is it?

☐ an herbal tea

☐ a sweet and sour main dish

☐ a refreshing drink

All you need to make this recipe is a sharp knife, a blender, and these ingredients: one lemon, sugar, ice, and four basil leaves. And if you don't have any basil, you can use rosemary or a little Tabasco sauce.

B **13 Write and listen again.** Fill in eight verbs to complete the conversation. Then listen to check your ideas.

> put   start   mix   cut   add   pour   peel   serve

Ethan: Anyway, here's what you do. First, _____ the lemon and _____ it into quarters.

Kirsten: Quarters—that means into four pieces?

Ethan: Exactly. Next, _____ the pieces of lemon in a blender along with some sugar. _____ some ice cubes, a liter of water, and the basil. Then _____ the blender and _____ it all at high speed for roughly 45 seconds.

Kirsten: Hey, that sounds easy.

Ethan: Yeah, it is. Finally, _____ the lemonade into glasses, and _____.

C Speak. What cooking tools and ingredients do you need to make these dishes? Work with a partner.

1. tuna sandwich   **2.** omelet   **3.** vegetable soup   **4.** Your idea: _____

Example:
A: What do you need to make a tuna sandwich?
B: You need a knife and a mixing bowl. I use a spatula, too.

frying pan
wooden spoon
spatula
whisk
knife
pot
mixing bowl

Working on Language ▶ Giving Instructions

Baked Bananas

First, peel three bananas.
Next, mix the bananas with some lemon juice, honey, and melted butter.
Then, bake the bananas for 15 minutes.
While the bananas are baking, melt some chocolate.
Finally, pour the melted chocolate over the bananas and serve.

A Read and write. Read the recipe and number the pictures in the order you do the activities. Then write the cooking verbs.

Pasta Fasol
Here's an easy recipe for pasta fasol, an Italian soup with tomatoes, onions, beans, and noodles.

First, **chop** an onion and some garlic into small pieces. Next, put some olive oil in a large pot, and **fry** the onion and garlic until soft. Then, **add** two cans of tomatoes and a can of bean soup. **Cook** on low heat for 15 minutes. While that's cooking, **boil** some water in another pot and prepare one cup of noodles. Finally, **drain** the noodles, and then **stir** them into the soup.

☐ _____

☐ _____

1 _chop_

☐ _____

☐ _____

☐ _____

☐ _____

B Speak. Give some cooking instructions to a partner. Your partner will act them out.

Example:
First, put some butter in a hot frying pan. Then, crack two eggs and put them in the pan.

Communicate ▶ What Do You Think?

A Write. Read these questions about food and write at least four more questions of your own. When you finish, share your ideas with your classmates.

> *Examples:* What's the strangest food you've ever eaten?
>
> What dish *do you want* to learn how to cook?
>
> Who's the best cook you know?
>
> 1.
>
> 2.
>
> 3.
>
> 4.

B Speak. Ask questions in groups. Write down the most interesting answers you hear.

Example:

Ethan: Who's the best cook you know, Sang-mi?

Sang-mi: My sister.

Ethan: What's the most delicious dish she makes?

Sang-mi: She makes really good *chijimi*.

Ethan: *Chijimi*? What's that?

Sang-mi: It's a Korean dish, sort of like a pizza.

Ethan: What's in it?

Sang-mi: Seafood usually, but she uses hamburger.

Student name	What did he/she say?
Sang-mi	Her sister puts hamburger in chijimi instead of seafood.

Working on Fluency ▶ Getting a Speaker to Slow Down

A 🔘 **14** **Listen.** A TV chef is explaining how to cook a Filipino dish. Check [✔] the dish that the chef describes.

1. ☐   2. ☐   3. ☐   4. ☐

B 🔘 **14** **Listen again.** Circle the three things the TV show host says to get the chef to slow down.

- Just a second.
- Wait a second.
- Hold on.

- Wait a minute.
- Hang on.
- Just a moment.

C Speak. Read one of these recipes to a partner. Your partner will close his/her book, take notes, and ask you to slow down when necessary.

💡 **Critical Thinking**

Think about how you can ask someone in a more polite way to slow down. For example, "Could you say that again, please?" Write two polite ways to slow someone down.

Western Omelet
For this recipe, you need a whisk, a mixing bowl, and a frying pan.
- First, crack three large eggs in a bowl and beat them with a whisk.
- Next, chop up an onion, a pepper, and some ham into small pieces. Add this to the egg mixture, and fry.

Banana Smoothie
For this recipe, you need a knife, a chopping board, and a blender.
- First, chop two bananas into small pieces and put them in a blender.
- Next, add some yogurt, some honey, and two cups of milk.
- Put the blender on high speed for one minute.

Example:

A: First, crack three large eggs in a bowl and beat them with a whisk.

B: Hold on. Did you say three **large** eggs?

A: Yes, I did. Next, chop up an onion . . .

Challenge

Make an unusual recipe and tell your classmates about it.

A Write. Think of three interesting dishes and complete the chart. Then tell a partner about them.

An unusual dish I have made:	*Example:* apple soup **Your idea:**
One of my favorite dishes:	*Example:* hamburger and fries **Your idea:**
My own original dish:	*Example:* beer-fried noodles **Your idea:**

Example:

A: What's your unusual dish?

B: Apple soup.

A: What's that?

B: It's a sweet soup from England.

B Write. Choose one dish and complete the class cookbook form on the next page.

C Speak. Practice explaining your recipe to a partner.

Example:

A: Here's an unusual old dish from England called "apple soup." To make it, you'll need a sharp knife, a cooking pot, and these ingredients: six apples, honey . . .

B: It sounds interesting. Is it easy to make?

A: Yes, it is. Here's how you do it. First, . . .

D Present. Describe your dish to your classmates and explain how to make it. Whose dishes would you like to try? Whose dishes wouldn't you like to try? Why or why not?

Level Up!
See page 72.

CLASS COOKBOOK

Chef's Name

Draw your dish here.

Here's a fast and easy / healthy / traditional / exotic dish called . . .

_____

To make it you'll need . . .

And these ingredients . . .

Here's how you do it . . .

Reflection Time

Write useful words and ideas you learned in this unit.

When You Have Time ▶ Extra Activities

If you finish an activity in this unit before your classmates, try one of these.

A Do the cooking utensils crossword puzzle.

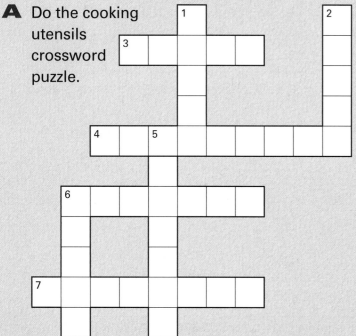

Across

3. A metal kitchen tool used to beat eggs or cream.

4. A type of oven that cooks food quickly without fire or flame.

6. The tool you use to turn things over in a frying pan.

7. A bowl that has many holes in it, used to wash or drain food.

Down

1. A kitchen clock that you set to ring to tell when a food is done.

2. A sharp tool you use to cut something.

5. You cut things on top of a ___ board.

6. The tool you use to stir things.

B Do the food history quiz.

1. Coca-Cola   **4.** Powdered milk
2. Cheesecake   **5.** Pizza
3. Chewing gum

_____ A cake made to feed Greek Olympic athletes in 776 B.C.

_____ This was made in Italy after Columbus brought tomatoes back from America.

_____ Marco Polo found Kubla Khan and the Mongols using this for instant food.

_____ This drink was first sold as a headache medicine.

_____ This candy, called Tutti Frutti, was sold in a vending machine in 1888.

C Talk with a partner about food and cooking.

1. Where do you shop for groceries?

2. What kind of snack foods do you like/dislike?

3. When you have to make something to eat in a hurry, what do you make?

4. When friends come over, what kind of food, snacks, and drinks do you usually prepare?

Level Up

Use these words to explain amounts in your recipes.

What food items can you buy in these containers? Add two more items to each list.

Container	Food
a bag of	rice
a bottle of	ketchup
a box of	noodles
a carton of	orange juice
a can of	beans

What food items would you use with these measurements? Add two more items to each list.

Measurement	Food
a cup of	sugar
a handful of	nuts
a pinch of	salt
a slice of	cheese
a spoonful of	soy sauce

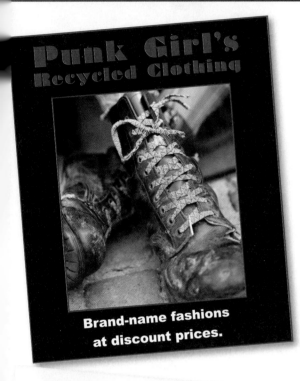

Punk Girl's Recycled Clothing

Brand-name fashions at discount prices.

Just Like Home

Only one dish each day, just like mom makes.

Rent-a-Pet

Why own a pet when you can rent one of ours?

Warm Up

A Number. What do you think about these business ideas? Rank them from 1 (the best) to 4 (the worst).

_____ Punk Girl's Recycled Clothing shop
_____ Just Like Home restaurant
_____ Rent-a-Pet
_____ Skateboard Delivery Service

B Speak. Ask some classmates what they think about the business ideas.

Example:
A: What do you think about Rent-a-Pet?
B: Well, it seems like a good idea. I gave it a "2."
A: Why's that?
B: I'd really like to have a pet, but not every day.

Skateboard Delivery Service

No other delivery service is as fast.

Challenge Preview

A  15 Listen.

In the *Challenge*, Luis is explaining his idea for an Asian restaurant. What kind of business is it?

☐ This restaurant only serves Chinese food.

☐ Each table has a different cuisine.

☐ This restaurant serves organic food.

> Hello. What kind of business is this?

B 15 Write and listen again. Fill in the blanks with *a*, *an*, or *the* to complete the conversation. Then listen to check your ideas.

Luis: Well, it's _____ Asian restaurant called East World.

Sang-mi: Hmm. There are a lot of Asian restaurants around here. What's special about this one?

Luis: Well, each table in _____ restaurant is shaped like _____ different country: Korea, Japan, China, and Thailand.

Sang-mi: I see.

Luis: You decide which cuisine you want to eat and sit at that table. For example, if you want to eat some Chinese food, sit at _____ Chinese table.

Sang-mi: Right. And if you want _____ Korean meal, you sit at _____ table shaped like Korea.

C Speak. What do you think each of these businesses do? Are they stores, schools, restaurants, or something else? Discuss them with a partner.

Example:

A: What kind of business is this?

B: I think it's a place to get married.

A: Maybe. I think it's . . .

Working on Language ▶ Explaining Key Features

What kind of business is it?	It's a low-cost airline that sells tickets only on its website.
How does it work?	You book tickets online and choose your own seat.
What's special about it?	There's one lucky seat on every flight. If you choose that seat, you pay only $1.

A **Write.** Complete these conversations, then practice with a partner.

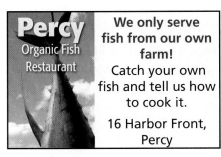

A: What kind of business is it?

B: _____

A: How does it work?

B: _____

A: What's special about it?

B: It's totally organic.

A: What kind of business is it?

B: _____

A: How does it work?

B: _____

A: What's special about it?

B: You don't have to get changed to try on your clothes.

B **Write.** Think of three shops or restaurants near your school. Make notes, like the example below. Don't show your partner.

Business name	Notes
Stone Cold	It's an ice cream shop near campus. They have more than 100 flavors. Mari works there.

C **Speak.** Describe your businesses to a partner. Your partner will guess the names of all the businesses.

Example:

A: It's an ice cream shop near campus.

B: Is it that place in the mall?

A: No, it's not. They have more than 100 flavors. Mari works there.

B: Is it Stone Cold?

A: That's right.

Communicate ▶ Business Think Tank

A **Read.** What can Joe's Burgers do to get more customers? Read these suggestions and add one more of your own.

Have a Joe's Burger today!

I think they need a better product. They could add some new hamburgers to their menu—like an extra-small diet burger.

They should advertise the business and give out free hamburger coupons at the train station.

I think they need a new name. How about changing their name to "World's Best Burgers?"

Your idea: _____

_____

_____

_____

B **Discuss.** Get into groups. Choose one business below (or a business you know). Think of ways this business can get more customers. Take notes.

Ideas to discuss: name, products, advertising, location, service

Egg Heaven

Egg Heaven serves breakfast only, open weekdays from 8:30 a.m. to 10 a.m.

Daily Roast sells only high-quality coffee, and nothing else.

ROCK

Rock specializes in rock music. It sells rock music on vinyl.

City Rider

City Rider buses are a little old, but the tickets are inexpensive.

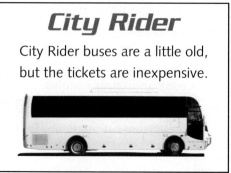

Working on Fluency ▶ Hesitating

A 🔘 **16** **Listen.** Mr. Lee is being interviewed about his chain of travel agencies, Easy Paradise. What makes his company successful?

☐ They have more than 600 branches.

☐ They organize tours all over the world.

☐ They offer a money-back guarantee.

☐ They are making an announcement soon.

B 🔘 **16** **Listen again.** Circle the four expressions Mr. Lee uses to hesitate and give himself some time to think.

- Let me see.
- Well, . . .
- I guess . . .

- Actually . . .
- Hmm . . .
- Let's just say . . .

C **Write and speak.** Talk with a partner about one of these topics or another of your own. Try to speak without any silences, using the hesitation expressions. Your partner will ask questions.

▸ a restaurant you like

▸ a website you enjoy

▸ a store you really like

▸ a movie you enjoyed/didn't enjoy

💡 **Critical Thinking**

Think about other phrases you can use, and things you can do, to give yourself time to think and avoid silences when speaking. List at least three ideas and use them when doing activity C.

Example:

A: One of my favorite stores is Pink Rabbit. It's, hmm, in the mall.

B: What kind of store is it?

A: Let me see. It's an interior design shop with, well, lots of great stuff.

B: What do you like about it? . . .

Challenge

With a partner, create a business plan for an original store, restaurant, or service. Explain your idea at a business fair, and try to get other students to invest in (give money to) your idea.

A Write. Brainstorm ideas for a new business. Choose one idea and complete the chart.

Business Type: shop / restaurant / service	Business Name: _____
What kind of business is it?	
How does your business work?	
What's special about it?	

B Write and speak. Make a floor plan, a list of services or products, or any other information you need. Practice explaining your business idea.

Level Up!
See page 80.

EAST WORLD

China
KOREA
BAR
Entrance
Thailand
Japan
Restrooms
Manager's table

Green Curry $8
Papaya Salad $4
Sticky Rice with Mango $4
Thai Ice Coffee $2

C Speak. Hold a business fair like this:

Partner A:
Luis

Partner B:
Ana

1. Display the information you prepared.

2. While one partner explains the business, the other partner visits other stores.

3. Later, change roles.

D Vote. Which business did you like best? Imagine you have $1 million. Where are you going to invest your money? Name the business.

I will invest $1 million in _____
because _____
_____.

Reflection Time

Write useful words and ideas you learned in this unit.

When You Have Time ▶ Extra Activities

If you finish an activity in this unit before your classmates, try one of these.

A Do the crossword puzzle.

```
[1][2][ ][3][ ][ ][ ]
      [ ]        [4]
      [ ]        [ ]
      [ ]  [5][ ][ ][ ][ ]
      [ ]        [ ]
      [ ]  [6][ ] [ ]
   [7][ ][ ][ ][ ][ ]
            [ ]
         [8][ ][ ][ ][ ][ ]
```

Across

1. A computer _____ makes computers.
5. You can find lawyers in a law _____.
7. Hotels, restaurants, and travel companies are part of the _____ industry.
8. A travel _____ is a place to buy tickets.

Down

2. A secretary works in an _____.
3. A book _____ makes books.
4. An _____ has flights to many places.
6. A tour _____ takes a group of people on a tour.

B Do the business quiz. True or false?

1. _____ The first 15 million cars made by Ford Motor Company were all black.
2. _____ The refrigerator was invented by Dr. Jack Frost in 1851.
3. _____ Barbie and Ken dolls were named after the inventor's two children.
4. _____ The first glass-making business operated 3,500 years ago in Mesopotamia.
5. _____ When Coco Chanel invented a perfume, she called it "Chanel No. 5" because five was her lucky number.

C Talk with a partner about businesses.

1. What are five businesses you often use (e.g., bank, transportation, Internet)?
2. Which one do you think has the best/worst service?
3. What business has really good advertisements?
4. What's the biggest business in your neighborhood?

Level Up

Use this sales technique to promote your business.

Ask a question	Answer the question
Are you in a hurry?	Then try Skateboard Delivery Service! We can help!
Do you need some new clothes?	Well, Punk Girl's Recycled Clothing is just what you're looking for!

Write a question and answer like the example above to promote these businesses. Then compare with a partner.

1. an ice cream shop called "Stone Cold"

_____

2. a pet rental company called "Rent-a-Pet"

_____

3. a travel agency called "Easy Paradise"

_____

4. a restaurant called "Just Like Home"

_____

5. a fast-food restaurant called "Joe's Burgers"

_____

Job Interview 9

Unit Challenge

▸ Role-play a job interview.
▸ Ask and answer job interview questions.

Warm Up

A Circle. Think about your job preferences and circle your choices.

I'd prefer to work:
- alone / with other people.
- at home / in an office / outdoors.
- in the city / in a small town.
- with my hands / using my head.
- from 9 to 5 / flexible hours.

B Speak. Compare your answers with a partner.

Example:
A: Would you prefer to work alone or with other people?
B: With other people.
A: Really? I'd rather work alone.

Challenge Preview

A 🔘 **17 Listen.**

In the *Challenge*, Luis is being interviewed for a new job. Which statement describes Luis?

☐ He is a creative person.

☐ He wants to work in an office.

☐ He'd rather work alone.

Well, my friends say I'm a pretty logical person.

OK, Mr. Garcia, can you tell us a little bit about yourself?

Logical?

B 🔘 **17 Write and listen again.** Fill in the missing words with *some* or *any* to complete the conversation. Then listen again to check your ideas.

Luis: Well, I like solving problems, and I'm good with numbers.

Ana: That's good. We're looking for interior designers to work in our office. They need to know how to use a computer. Do you have _____ computer experience, Mr. Garcia?

Luis: Absolutely. I took _____ computer classes in college, and I use a computer a lot at home.

Ana: That's great. Do you know how to use _____ computer-assisted design programs?

Luis: Well, I've used _____ of them, and I'm sure I can learn how to use _____ software you have. That's no problem.

C Speak. Ask a partner to describe himself/herself. Then change roles.

Example:
A: OK, Jerry, can you tell me a little bit about yourself?
B: Well, my friends say I'm a pretty creative person.
A: Creative?
B: Well, I like making things, and I'm quite good at drawing.

Working on Language ▸ Describing Job Requirements

> I think an office manager . . .
> ▸ **has to** be well organized.
> ▸ **needs to** be able to motivate others.
>
> Also, he/she . . .
> ▸ **should** have a college degree.
> ▸ **ought to** know how to use a computer.

A Write. Complete the sentences about these jobs. Then compare your answers with other students.

1. I think a taxi driver has to

_____

_____ .

Also, he ought to

_____

_____ .

2. A bank manager needs to

_____

_____ .

Also, he should

_____

_____ .

3. A radio DJ

_____

_____ .

Also, she

_____

_____ .

B Discuss. What skills are needed for these jobs? Discuss with a partner.

> a tour guide   a chef   a kindergarten teacher   a company president

Example:
A: I think a tour guide needs to have good people skills.
B: Yeah, that's true. Also, a tour guide has to know a lot about culture and history.

Level Up!
See page 88.

C Speak. How good would you be at the jobs on this page? Discuss with a partner.

Example:
A: I don't think I'd be a good kindergarten teacher. A kindergarten teacher has to be patient, and I'm not patient at all.
B: Me neither! How about a chef? Do you think you'd be good at that?
A: Yeah, I like cooking. I can make a meal out of anything.

Communicate ▶ What's Your Ideal Job?

A Write. Finish the survey below by writing two more questions for each skill area.

JOB SKILLS SURVEY

Organizing Skills (e.g. planning, finding things out, scheduling, taking notes)

1. Do you like planning parties or events?
2. Are you good at finding information on the Internet?
3. _____
4. _____

People Skills (e.g. communicating, understanding, being a leader)

5. Are you a good listener?
6. Do others sometimes ask for your ideas and advice?
7. _____
8. _____

Thinking Skills (e.g. solving problems, discussing ideas, making decisions)

9. Do you like solving puzzles?
10. Do you like mystery novels or movies?
11. _____
12. _____

B Speak and write. Use your survey to interview three classmates. Decide what each person's strongest skill area is and suggest an ideal job for each person. Share your ideas with the class.

Example:
A: Do you like planning parties or events?
B: Yes, I do. I'm pretty good at it. I helped plan my friend's wedding.

> Yumi has strong organization skills. I think she would be a good wedding planner or event coordinator.

Student Name	Strongest Skill Area	Ideal Jobs
Yumi	organization skills	wedding planner, event coordinator

Working on Fluency ▶ "Mirroring" the Speaker's Words

A 🔘 **18** **Listen.** Ms. Lopez is being interviewed for a new job. Check [✔] the job she wants.

☐ Internet researcher

☐ Web designer

☐ newsletter editor

☐ digital photographer

B 🔘 **18** **Listen again.** The interviewer repeats some of Ms. Lopez's own words as a question—he "mirrors" her—to get her to say more. Circle the three questions he asks.

- Multimedia center?
- Our company?
- Impressed?

- Photography classes?
- A new design?
- Computer classes?

> **💡 Critical Thinking**
>
> Which of these questions gets the speaker to say more. Why?
>
> **1. a.** Did you like high school?
> **b.** How was high school for you?
>
> **2. a.** What do you want to be in the future?
> **b.** What kind of career are you thinking about?
>
> Write a question you think will get a speaker to say a lot about his/her hobbies.

C **Speak.** Talk about each topic with a partner for as long as possible. Your partner will mirror your words.

▶ a class you enjoyed

▶ a person you like

▶ a job you had

▶ a hobby you have or had

Example:

A: Last year, I took an interesting business class.

B: An interesting business class?

A: Yes. It was about business in China . . .

Challenge

Your company needs to find new staff. Interview your classmates to find the best applicants for the jobs below.

A Read. Get into small groups (ideally, groups of three) and choose a company—"IDK Advertising Co." or "Dream House Co." There should be an equal number of groups for both companies. Read about your group's company.

IDK Advertising Co.
Your company produces TV commercials.
There are openings for:
- actors/actresses.
- film directors.
- scriptwriters.

Dream House Co.
Your company designs and sells houses.
There are openings for:
- project managers.
- interior designers.
- salespeople.

B Speak and write. What skills are needed for your company's job openings? Think of interview questions to check for these skills. Read the example and complete the chart.

Example:

A: A scriptwriter should have good writing skills. We can ask something like, "Were you good at writing school reports?"

B: Good idea. They also need to be creative. We could ask about that, too.

Job	Important skills	Interview questions
scriptwriter	• good writing skills	• How did you do on papers you wrote for school?

C Speak. Pair up with another group that has a different company from yours. Interview the members from that group. Take notes on each person's answers.

> Tell us about yourself, Yumi. Why would you like to work for us?

Name and Personal Information:

Yumi / 20 years old / English major

Skills and Experience:

good communication skills / very friendly /

has worked in department store for two years

Best job for this person:

salesperson

Notes

_____
_____
_____
_____
_____
_____
_____

D Speak. Discuss which job each applicant should get and why. Then tell your decisions to the other group.

> Yumi has good communication skills, and she's very friendly. Also, she has been working in a department store for two years. I think we should hire her as one of our salespeople.

Presentation Tip

Connect your interview answers to the company's needs, so that you sound like a problem-solver rather than just job hunter.
Example: "That story I wrote is the kind of writing I can do for you."

Reflection Time

Write useful words and ideas you learned in this unit.

When You Have Time ▶ Extra Activities

If you finish an activity in this unit before your classmates, try one of these.

A Rank these real jobs from 1 (the strangest) to 6 (the least strange).

_____ A **chicken sexer** looks at newborn baby chicks to sort them into male and female groups.

_____ A **recliner checker** sits in new chairs to see whether they are comfortable.

_____ An **ice cream taster** eats three cartons of ice cream a day to check quality.

_____ A **snake milker** collects deadly poison from snakes' fangs.

_____ A **joyologist** is a psychologist who helps people laugh more for better health.

_____ A **hacker tracker** hunts people who make computer viruses.

B Do the classmates quiz. Who do you think:

- would be a good class leader?
  _____

- is the best communicator?
  _____

- is a good problem-solver?
  _____

- is a great organizer?
  _____

- is the toughest interviewer?
  _____

- Your idea: _____
  _____

C Talk with a partner about jobs.

1. What was the first job you ever had?
2. What was the best job you ever had? Why?
3. What was the worst job you ever had? Why?
4. What job would you like to have?

Level Up

You can talk about job requirements using "shouldn't be" + a negative adjective and "shouldn't have" + a noun phrase.

Examples:
An office manager should be organized.

▶ An office manager shouldn't be disorganized.

A taxi driver should have a good sense of direction.

▶ A taxi driver shouldn't have a bad sense of direction.

Write sentences using phrases such as those above to describe a requirement for these jobs.

1. a doctor / impatient:
_____
_____

2. a dancer / bad sense of rhythm:
_____
_____

3. a kindergarten teacher / too strict:
_____
_____

4. an office manager / unable to motivate others:
_____
_____

5. Your idea:
_____
_____

Job Fair

Research a job you would like to have, and make a poster for it. Then hold a job fair with the whole class.

A Discuss. These students are talking about their dream jobs. Which job would you like to do the most?

I think it would be interesting to be a soccer coach in a high school, like my friend's mother. I'm going to talk to her about how I could get a job like that.

I want to design computer games, but I don't like programming. I'm going to use the Internet to find some game companies and what kinds of game development jobs there are.

I'd like to have my own pet shop for dogs. I'm going to read some business and dog shop magazines to find out how to start a business like that.

B Prepare. Choose a job you would like to know more about. Write what you need to know about this job and where you might find that information.

Job:	
What I need to find out:	**Where I can get the information:**

C **Create.** Make a poster for the job you researched. Include at least four topics like those in the example below.

Job: Computer Game AI Developer

What it is: A Computer Game AI Developer usually works with simulation games, such as real-time fantasy or war games. This person decides the story, and what actions the computer will do while playing. The computer has to have its own game strategy and know how to react to anything the "human" player does.

Companies where such jobs exist:
- Microsoft
- Electronic Arts
- Sony
- Activision

Salary:
$40,000 – $120,000 a year, but very long hours

Requirements:
- any college degree
- love for games and knowledge about most popular games
- understanding of computers and systems software
- ability to work in teams and for long hours

Where to search for jobs:
1. On the Internet, search for "computer games AI developer jobs."
2. Attend a game developers conference.

D **Speak.** Hold a job fair. Put all the posters around the room. Then take turns standing next to your poster or walking around the room asking other students questions.

Example:
A: What does the "AI" mean in "Computer Game AI Developer"?
B: "AI" means "artificial intelligence." It means how the computer thinks in a game.
A: Do you have to be a programmer to get this job?
B: No. It helps if you know something about programming, but you don't have to be a programmer.

Unit Challenge

▸ Write a short scene for a TV show or movie.
▸ Perform it in front of the class.

Warm Up

A **Write.** How much time do you spend watching TV and movies?

Watching TV: _____ hours a day

Watching videos online: _____ hours a week

Watching videos on a cell phone or portable media player: _____ hours a week

Seeing movies in theaters: _____ times a year

Renting movies: _____ times a month

B **Speak.** Ask your classmates about these activities.

Example:
A: Do you watch much TV?
B: Yes, about three hours a day.

Challenge Preview

A 🔘 **19 Listen.**

In the *Challenge*, some students are acting out a TV preview. What kind of show is it?

☐ It's a documentary.

☐ It's a quiz show.

☐ It's a news program.

> Will Jessica be able to answer the professor's tough questions and win $1 million? Let's watch.

Jessica

B 🔘 **19 Write and listen again.** Fill in five phrases to complete the conversation. One phrase is not used. Then listen to check your ideas.

| I give up! | Let me see. | That's right! | Not really. | Come on. | I've got it! |

Steven: OK, Jessica. Here's the first question. What's the longest word in the English language?

Ana: _____ I don't know. The longest word. Oh dear.

Steven: _____ You can do it, Jessica. Think about it. What's the longest word?

Ana: _____ I'm really sorry but I just don't know.

Steven: Don't give up, Jessica. Give me a big smile. Jessica, that's a hint.

Ana: _____ The longest word in the English language is "smiles."

Steven: _____ Congratulations! Now, for $10,000, can you tell us why?

Ana: I sure can! The longest word is "smiles" because there's a "mile" between the first and last letters.

Steven: That's right. Congratulations!

C Speak. Ask a partner what movies or TV shows he/she likes to watch.

Example:

A: How do you feel about quiz shows?

B: I love them! I watch them all the time.

Types of shows

documentary, music show, quiz show, reality TV show, sitcom, soap opera, talk show, the news, variety show

Types of movies

action, comedy, fantasy, historical, drama, horror, romance, science fiction

---

Working on Language ▶ Describing What Something Is About

What it is	**More information**
24 is a TV series about a guy who tries to stop terrorists.	There are 24 episodes. Each episode is one hour. Together, they make one day.
Infernal Affairs is a crime thriller that is set in Hong Kong.	Andy Lau plays Inspector Lau Kin Ming, one of the main characters.
The Oprah Winfrey Show is an extremely popular talk show.	Oprah is the host, and she always has interesting guests.

A Write. Think of some movies and TV shows you have seen, like the examples. Write sentences about them to use in a quiz game.

action movie, actor/actress, the bad guys, a big hit

reality TV show, presenter, contestants, the winner

Example: It's a movie about a superhero who fights bad guys. It's based on a comic book series.

1. _____

2. _____

3. _____

B Speak. Use your sentences and do a quiz. Read your sentences. Your classmates will ask you *yes*/*no* questions until they guess the show.

Example:

A: It's a movie about a superhero who fights bad guys. It's based on a comic book series.
B: Can the superhero fly?
A: No, he can't.
B: Does the main character wear a red suit?
A: Yes.
B: Is it *Spiderman*?
A: That's right!

Level Up!
See page 98.

Communicate ▶ What's Your Favorite?

A **Write.** What are some questions you would like to ask your classmates about TV and movies? Use these or your own ideas. Then share your ideas with your classmates.

past and present favorites?

recommendations?

likes and dislikes?

actors and presenters?

awards?

Example: <u>What was your favorite TV show when you were a child? What was it about?</u>

1. _____

2. _____

3. _____

B **Speak.** Get into groups. Ask classmates questions. If you hear something interesting, write it down.

Example:

A: Kristi, what's a movie that you really like?

B: Hmm. Let me see. Maybe *High School Musical.*

A: What do you like about it?

B: I love the songs, and Ashley Tisdale is really funny.

Student	Movie
Kristi	*High School Musical,* Ashley Tisdale

Working on Fluency ▶ Speaking Dramatically

A 💿 **20 Listen.** Steven and Sang-mi are watching TV, flipping through some TV channels. Number the pictures to show the order in which they see each preview.

a. ☐

b. ☐

c. ☐

B 💿 **20 Listen again.** Write the way each character's voice sounds. Use the words in the box or your own ideas.

> nervous   romantic   strict   happy   tough   bored

1. The comedy: Jenny: _____   Jenny's mom: _____
2. The spy movie: Jack: _____   His enemy: _____
3. The drama: Mandy: _____   Josh: _____

C **Speak.** Act out these three movie scenes in the chart with a partner using the script below. Put drama into your voice.

Script:

A: Please get in the car.
B: I . . . I . . .
A: Let's go!
B: No, I can't.

A: What's wrong?
B: I want to stay here.
A: But we have to go now . . .

> 💡 **Critical Thinking**
>
> Think about how your body and facial expressions convey meaning. Practice the movie scenes again, changing the way you stand and move your body, and changing your facial expressions.

Movie	Partner A	Partner B
Martial arts movie: *Kick Master II*	Kick Master's friend: scared The bad guys are coming. You want to escape.	The Kick Master: tough You aren't afraid of the bad guys. You want to fight.
Horror movie: *Vampire*	Dracula: dangerous You are hungry for blood.	Victim: scared You think this person might be a vampire.
Teen romance: *First Love*	Teen boy: romantic You want to take your date somewhere romantic.	Teen girl: nervous You want to go, but you are afraid your parents will be angry.

Challenge

Make a preview of a TV show or movie and act it out. It should have an introduction and one scene.

A Discuss. Work in groups. Think of a real or made-up TV show (or movie) you want to advertise. Write its name.

Name of movie/TV show: _____

B Write. Prepare a preview for your show: write an introduction and one short scene. Use the example below to help you.

Your introduction should include:
- When and where to see the show.
- What it's about.
- Why people should watch it.

Kirsten (Announcer): Tonight. At 7 p.m. Don't miss the exciting new episode of *Million Dollar Student*, the quiz show filmed in a real English classroom. Will Jessica be able to answer the professor's tough questions and win $ 1 million? Let's watch.

Short scene:
Steven (presenter) and Ana (Jessica, the contestant)

Steven: OK, Jessica. Here's the first question. What's the longest word in the English language?

Ana: Let me see. I don't know. The longest word. Oh dear.

Steven: Come on. You can do it, Jessica. Think about it. What's the longest word?

C Prepare. Practice your preview. Think about:

▶ where to stand.

▶ how to move.

▶ facial expressions and gestures.

▶ how to speak dramatically.

▶ timing.

D Perform. Act out your preview at the front of the class. The other students will evaluate your group and write comments on separate pieces of paper.

Group 1	Notes
Name and type of show	*Million Dollar Student—quiz show*
Idea	*Great idea for a show. I'd love to watch this.*
Pronunciation/Delivery	*Volume was OK. But speaking was sometimes too fast.*
Acting	*Everyone's acting was good, but Ana's acting was perfect.*

Optional Activity: Have a movie awards ceremony. Think of awards as a class, e.g., Best Actor, Best Actress, Best Narrator, Best Drama Scene, Best Preview Idea, etc. Then make groups and decide the winners.

Presentation Tip

While you are on stage and waiting your turn to speak, try to look like you are listening and very interested in what the current speaker is saying.

Reflection Time

Write useful words and ideas you learned in this unit.

When You Have Time ▶ Extra Activities

If you finish an activity in this unit before your classmates, try one of these.

A Do the movie genre crossword.

Across

1. Scary monsters appear in ___ movies.
3. Soldiers fight battles in ___ movies.
5. Wizards, hobbits, and elves appear in ___ movies.
6. A murder mystery movie is called a ___.
7. You may laugh till it hurts if you see a ___.

Down

2. A love story is called a ___.
3. If the star wears cowboy boots, it's a ___.
4. A movie with a lot of singing is a ___.

B Do the movie quiz. Match the movies to their advertising taglines.

1. *Finding Nemo* •
2. *Braveheart* •
3. *Harry Potter* •
4. *War of the Worlds* •
5. *Titanic* •
6. *Lord of the Rings* •

- Magic will happen.
- They're already here.
- Sea it.
- Every man dies, not every man really lives.
- Power can be held in the smallest of things . . .
- Nothing on Earth could come between them.

C Talk with a partner about media.

1. Do you read books, newspapers, magazines, or material online?
2. Which ones do you like? Why?
3. When and where do you read?
4. Are you interested in the news? Why or why not?

Level Up

Use relative clauses to give more information about a movie, TV show, actor, or director. Complete these sentences with a relative pronoun: *who* or *that*.

1. I really enjoy watching the Japanese cartoon called *Shin Chan*. It's a TV show about a little boy _____ always gets into trouble.
2. *Titanic* is a movie about a ship _____ hits an iceberg and sinks. Leonardo DiCaprio plays Jack, the main character.
3. I love to watch *American Idol*. In this reality show, it's the judges (and not the contestants) _____ are the real stars of the show.
4. *Ratatouille* is an animated movie about a rat _____ wants to be a chef in a top Parisian restaurant.
5. I'll watch anything directed by Quentin Tarantino. He's a director _____ always makes really interesting movies.

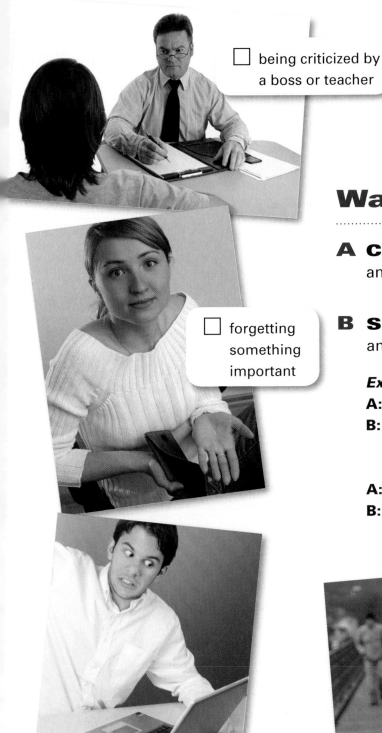

☐ being criticized by a boss or teacher

☐ forgetting something important

☐ buying something that turns out to be broken

☐ waiting for someone who is late

Unit Challenge

▸ Think of a dilemma and some possible solutions.
▸ Conduct a survey to find out what your classmates would do.

Warm Up

A **Check [✓].** Which of these things have annoyed you in the past?

B **Speak.** Tell a partner about some of the annoying things you've experienced.

Example:
A: What's an annoying thing that happened to you?
B: Well, I bought a new MP3 player about a month ago. I spent ages installing my entire music collection onto it, and then it broke.
A: That's terrible. What did you do?
B: I took it back to the shop, and now I have to install everything again. Argh!

Challenge Preview

A  **Listen.**

In the *Challenge*, Yumi is explaining a dilemma that her cousin is having.

☐ She's having a problem with her computer.

☐ She's had a fight with her boyfriend.

☐ She's having a problem with her parents.

[Speech bubbles in image:]
Hi Yumi. What's your dilemma?

OK, um, this story isn't about me—it's about my cousin.

B 21 **Write and listen again.** Fill in the correct form of the verbs to complete the conversation. Then listen to check your ideas.

Yumi: Fumi has (fall) _____ in love with someone she met online, and she says she's really in love with this guy. They chat a lot online, and they've (meet) _____ each other a few times. The guy seems really nice, and now they're (talk) _____ about getting married.

Sang-mi: So . . . what's the problem, then?

Yumi: Well, the problem is Fumi's parents. They are kind of old-fashioned, and they don't like the situation at all. They've (order) _____ Fumi to stop (talk) _____ to the guy and find a "real" boyfriend. So, here's my question: What would you do if you were Fumi?

Sang-mi: Hmm. Well, if I were Fumi, I'd probably talk to my parents and try to make them understand.

C **Speak.** What would you do in Fumi's situation? Read the examples and discuss with a partner.

If I were Fumi, I'd invite my parents to have dinner with this guy. They might change their minds if they got to know him.

If I were Fumi, I'd keep talking to this guy in secret. Sometimes it's better not to tell your parents everything.

If I were in that situation, I'd listen to my parents. My parents are usually right about things in the end.

May

Sue

Andrew

Working on Language ▶ Talking about Hypothetical Situations

A Write. Read about Ally's problem and the possible ways she could deal with it. Then, add an idea of your own.

Ally is a manager in a company. She is having dinner with an employee from her office when she realizes she doesn't have any money with her. **What would you do if you were Ally?**

- **If I were Ally, I'd** borrow money from my employee and pay her back later.
- **If I were in that situation, I'd** call a friend and ask for help.
- **If that happened to me, I'd** ask my employee to pay for the dinner.

Your idea: _____

_____

B Write. What would you do in these difficult situations?

1. Carlos' teacher always makes him sit next to someone he doesn't like.
   If I were Carlos, _____

2. After a busy day, Eve's friends show up at her door and want to have a party at her place.
   _____

3. After a day of shopping at the mall, Junko finds out she has locked her keys in the car.
   _____

4. Hoi-Kin wants to go to an all-night dance, but her mom wants her home by 10 p.m.
   _____

5. Peter's teacher keeps calling him by the wrong name.
   _____

C Speak. Compare your answers with a partner. Then, tell your classmates your best idea for each situation. Who has the most interesting solutions?

Example:
A: If I were Carlos, I'd tell the teacher about the problem.
B: That's one possibility, but if I were in that situation, I'd just move without saying anything.

Useful Expressions

That's one possibility, but . . .
To tell you the truth, . . .
That sounds good. I'd do that too.
I'm not sure, but . . .

Communicate ▶ What Would You Do?

A Speak. Choose four of these questions and discuss in groups. Think about what you would do and compare your answers.

Example:

A: OK, let's discuss the first situation. So what would you do, Lynn?

B: Well, if that happened to me, I'd try to find the owner. The dog is in danger, so it's better to act quickly. How about you, Frank?

C: That might work, but if I were in that situation, I'd break the window and let the dog out myself. I think it's wrong to leave an animal alone in a car.

1. Imagine you see a dog locked in a parked car on a hot summer day. The dog has no water, and it looks really hot.

4. Would you move to a distant country, far from friends and family, to be with someone you loved deeply?

2. Would you accept $1 million to never see or talk to your best friend again?

5. Imagine you have to make this choice: leaving your hometown forever or never being allowed to leave. What would you do and why?

3. Would you give money to a well-dressed stranger who says he lost his wallet and needs money to get home on a bus? Why or why not?

6. If you became the leader of your country, what's the first thing you would change, and why would you change it?

B Speak. How did people in your group respond? Tell your classmates.

Example:

A: Most people in our group said that they'd move to a distant country to be with a loved one. But one person said that he'd stay with his friends and family.

Level Up!
See page 106.

> ## Useful Expressions
>
> Everyone said that . . .
> Most people said that . . .
> A few people said that . . .
> One person said that . . .
> No one said that . . .

Working on Fluency ▶ Introducing Opinions

A 🔘 **22** **Listen.** The hosts of a radio talk show are discussing a news story. What's the story?

☐ A girl got angry when her brother ate her ice cream cone.

☐ A boy bought an ice cream cone but didn't buy one for his sister.

☐ There was something wrong with the girl's ice cream cone.

B 🔘 **22** **Listen again.** Circle the five phrases the speakers use to introduce their ideas.

- Just between you and me, . . .
- To be honest, . . .
- In my opinion, . . .
- I shouldn't say this, but . . .
- Frankly, . . .
- Personally, . . .

C Read and speak. Discuss these situations with a partner. Use the phrases from activity B to introduce your opinions.

1. A 40-year-old man asked police to arrest his wife because she sold his comic book collection to a used-book store. The man claimed he could live without his wife but not without his comics . . .

2. A woman sued a TV weatherman after he predicted a sunny day and it rained. The woman claimed she left home without an umbrella after watching the forecast. As a result, she caught the flu and . . .

3. A teacher was fined $10,000 for giving an eight-year-old student a "really bad haircut." The teacher claimed the boy's long hair was against school rules, but the boy's mother said . . .

> 💡 **Critical Thinking**
>
> Think about how the phrases in activity B tell the listener what kind of information will follow. Which of the phrases could be followed by:
> - a secret: "John quit his job."
> - a very different opinion: "You are completely wrong."

Example:

A: What do you think about the first situation?

B: To be honest, I think the man was right. I'd be pretty angry if it happened to me.

C: Well, frankly, I don't know. Maybe the wife really needed the money.

Challenge

Describe a dilemma, guess the most common response, and conduct a survey to check.

A Think and discuss. Read the dilemma and decide what you would do. Then find out how your classmates responded. How many said they'd do the same thing?

Dilemma

 OR

A classmate has been offered a great job in another city, but his parents have asked him to stay home and manage the restaurant they own. What would you do if you were in his situation?

☐ If I were in that situation, I'd take the job and try to make my parents understand.

☐ If I had to make that choice, I'd probably turn down the job and help my parents.

☐ Your idea: _____

B Write. Think of a dilemma and possible solutions. Then choose the answer you think most of your classmates will give.

Dilemma: _____

Possible solutions: _____

_____

The most common answer: _____

_____

C Speak and write. Explain your dilemma to as many classmates as possible. Make notes about their answers. Check [✔] the people who gave the same answer as you guessed in activity B.

Name	Answer	Same as my guess

D Speak. Share your results in groups.

My story was about a classmate. He was offered a job in a different city, but his parents wanted him to stay home and work in the family restaurant. I thought most people would say they'd take the job, but I was wrong. Only four people said they'd take the job. That was surprising.

Presentation Tip

Tell your story with short breaks between the phrases, rather than just between the sentences: "his parents . . . wanted him . . . to stay home."

Reflection Time

Write useful words and ideas you learned in this unit.

When You Have Time ▶ Extra Activities

If you finish an activity in this unit before your classmates, try one of these.

A Do the crossword puzzle.

Across

2. I shouldn't ___ this, but I don't like my job.

3. To be ___, I don't know.

4. What ___ you do if you got fired?

5. Sometimes it's ___ not to tell your parents.

6. That ___ good. I'd do that too.

Down

1. Just ___ you and me, I wouldn't do that.

2. What would you do if you were in that ___?

3. If that ___ to me, I'd just look for another job.

B Do the quiz. A survey asked these questions. How do you think people answered? Number the answers 1 (most popular) to 4 (least popular).

a. Do you believe in unending love?
___ Yes   ___ No

b. What if your partner cheated on you?
___ Leave him/her.   ___ Stay together.
___ Not sure.

c. If you could move to another country, where would you go?
___ I would stay here. ___ Italy
___ United States   ___ United Kingdom

d. What's the most important thing in a relationship?
___ respect   ___ attraction
___ interest   ___ communication

e. If you could be an animal, what would you be?
___ a lion   ___ a dolphin
___ a cat   ___ a dog

C Talk with a partner about these situations.

1. If you could have dinner with any famous person, who would it be? Why?

2. If you could be anyone in your class, who would you be?

3. If you could have a superpower (fly, travel through time, etc.), what would you choose?

4. If you could marry someone very, very rich and famous but you did not love the person, would you?

Level Up

When you use these words, remember that "everyone," "almost everyone," "not everyone," and "no one" are singular. "Most people" and "a few people" are plural.

Example:

I think *most people / only a few people* in my class **have** an MP3 player.

Write sentences about your classmates using the words above. Compare with a partner.

1. part-time job: _I think_ _____

2. punk music: _____

3. shopping: _____

4. TV: _____

5. your idea: _____

☐ It's impossible to become fluent in a foreign language without studying abroad.

Warm Up

A Check [✔]. What's your opinion? Check the statements you agree with.

B Speak. Tell a partner your opinion about the statements you checked.

Example:
A: I think it's impossible to become fluent in a foreign language without studying abroad.
B: Well, I think you can become fluent by studying hard.

☐ Cell phones should be banned in public places.

☐ Animals should not be kept in enclosed places.

☐ Grades should be based on daily work instead of exams.

Challenge Preview

A 🎵 **23 Listen.**
In the first part of the *Challenge*, Kirsten and Ethan are presenting their main points in a debate on downloading music illegally. Check [✔] the three points they mention.

These days, downloading music off the Internet without paying for it has become really common.

☐ It's wrong to take something without paying.

☐ Musicians should be paid for their work.

☐ There aren't many free music sites.

☐ It can damage your computer.

B 🎵 **23 Write and listen again.** Fill in the missing words with *nobody*, *somebody*, or *everybody* to complete the conversation. Then listen to check your ideas.

Kirsten: Let's look at the first point. It's stealing. I heard that _____ went to jail for downloading music without paying for it. I don't want to go to jail for downloading music illegally. Do you?

Ethan: Now let's talk about how illegal downloading hurts musicians. _____ makes music for free. It's a job. For example, when _____ records a song, he or she should be paid for it.

Kirsten: Seriously, _____ should support his or her favorite bands by buying music—not by stealing it! If _____ downloaded music illegally, bands wouldn't get any money. Without money, _____ would make new CDs. Do you want that to happen?

C Speak. What's your opinion? Do you agree or disagree with the points given in activity A? Discuss with a partner. Then share your ideas with your classmates.

Example:
A: To tell you the truth, I don't think there's anything wrong with downloading music for free.
B: I don't think so either. My friend recommended a band to me. I downloaded a few songs, and I loved them! A week later, I bought their CD.

Working on Language ▶ Making a Position Statement

In favor of:	I (personally) feel that	everybody should be required to study a foreign language.
	I (sincerely) believe that	
Against:	I (strongly) disagree that	
	I (seriously) doubt that	

A Write and speak. What's your position? Complete the sentences so they are true for you. Then compare with a partner.

1. _____ baseball is more exciting to watch than soccer.

2. _____ everyone in the world will speak English one day.

3. _____ global warming is the biggest problem the world faces today.

4. _____ playing violent video games leads to violent behavior.

5. _____ it's necessary to use animals for medical research.

6. _____ men are just as good at taking care of children as women are.

Example:

A: I personally feel that baseball is a more exciting game to watch than soccer.

B: I don't really agree. I believe that baseball players spend a lot of the time just standing around doing nothing.

> **Useful Expressions**
>
> I think so, too.
> I completely agree.
> I don't really agree.
> I completely disagree.
> I can't accept that.

B Write and speak. On a separate piece of paper, write four sentences stating your position on these topics or others of your own. Then take turns reading your sentences and comparing ideas.

> school uniforms   smoking   cell phones
> the government   fast food   the Internet

Example: I strongly disagree that fast-food restarants should be able to sell food in schools.

> I strongly disagree that fast-food restaurants should be able to sell food in schools.

> I agree with you. That would be terrible because . . .

Communicate ▶ Why Do You Think That?

A Read and write. Read this position statement and the supporting reasons. Add another reason of your own based on common knowledge, your experience, or a source.

Level Up!
See page 114.

Position Statement:
I strongly believe that smoking should be banned in public places.

Reasons

Common knowledge:
Everybody knows that second-hand smoke is dangerous.

Personal experience:
In my experience, smokers don't seem to care if other people have to breathe their smoke.

Reference to a source:
According to a TV show I saw, breathing second-hand smoke is actually just as harmful as smoking.

A reason of your own: _____

B Check [✓], write, and speak. Check your position on these issues and write a reason based on common knowledge, experience, or a source. Then compare in groups.

1. Dogs make better pets than cats.

☐ Agree   ☐ Disagree

Reason: _____

2. Students should not be allowed to use cell phones at school.

☐ Agree   ☐ Disagree

Reason: _____

3. It's better to work for a big company than for a small one.

☐ Agree   ☐ Disagree

Reason: _____

4. It's a waste of money to buy a designer bag.

☐ Agree   ☐ Disagree

Reason: _____

Working on Fluency ▶ Illustrating Your Point

A 🔘 **24** **Listen.** Steven and Ana are responding to the points made by Ethan and Kirsten. Check [✔] the types of reasons they give.

	Common knowledge	Experience	A source
1. Nobody has gone to jail for downloading.			
2. Bands make music because they love music.			
3. People who download songs often buy the CDs.			
4. Not many people get computer viruses.			

B 🔘 **24** **Listen again.** Circle four phrases Steven and Ana use to illustrate their points.

- Consider this.
- Let me tell you why.
- Here's something to think about.

- For example, . . .
- For instance, . . .
- For one thing, . . .

> ### 💡 Critical **Thinking**
> Think about what makes a strong point. Listen to track 24 again and rank the speakers' four points in activity A from 1 (the strongest) to 4 (the weakest).

C **Speak.** Discuss two of these statements with a partner using phrases from activity B. One person agrees, and the other doesn't. Then change roles.

▶ It's better to live alone than with your parents.

▶ Children should not be allowed to have TVs or computers in their rooms.

▶ All high school students should wear uniforms.

▶ Students should get paid for high grades.

Example:

A: I sincerely believe that it's better to live alone than with your parents. Let me tell you why. When you live alone, you can do what you want, when you want.

B: Well, I can't accept that. It's not good for you. Everybody knows that people who live with their parents have healthier lifestyles. For example, . . .

Challenge

Choose a position statement, prepare arguments, and have an informal group debate.

A **Speak and write.** In groups of four, brainstorm position statements that you think would make an interesting debate. List your three best ideas. Then, choose one.

Example: Downloading music without paying for it should be stopped.

Position statement idea 1:

Position statement idea 2:

Position statement idea 3:

B **Write and speak.** Make pairs. Decide which pair will agree with the statement and which will disagree. Work with your partner to complete the chart with at least three arguments.

Position statement to debate:

In favor ☐ **Against** ☐

Your reasons and examples:

C Hold a mini-debate. Work in your groups and follow these instructions:

1. Take turns presenting your arguments in pairs.
2. As you listen to the other pair, take notes.
3. Try to find weaknesses in their arguments.
4. Respond to their arguments.
5. Finally, decide which pair made the strongest arguments.

You said that soccer games are boring because there isn't much action. This is not true. Soccer games are very exciting because the play never stops.

Presentation Tip

Change your voice every few sentences to keep your speech interesting. Change the tone, pitch, speed, and loudness.

Reflection Time

Write useful words and ideas you learned in this unit.

When You Have Time ▸ Extra Activities

If you finish an activity in this unit before your classmates, try one of these.

A Do the word search. Find the missing words.

D	E	X	A	M	P	L	E
E	N	M	E	O	T	D	E
B	O	W	R	T	E	E	R
A	I	E	W	R	O	N	G
T	N	E	M	U	G	R	A
E	I	E	S	E	L	E	S
E	P	M	E	U	O	X	I
N	O	S	A	E	R	X	D

1. That's your o___. Mine is different.
2. Here's the r___ why I think I'm right.
3. Let's have a d___ and discuss this issue.
4. Your a___ has some mistakes in it.
5. Here's an e___ to illustrate my point.
6. You agree with the statement, but I d___.
7. What you just said isn't t___.
8. It's w___ to take something without paying.

B Everyday (but silly) debates. Do you agree, yes or no?

1. ___ Cups and glasses should be stored tops up, not down.
2. ___ You should never watch TV while eating a meal with your family.
3. ___ Men make better cooks than women.
4. ___ When you call someone, you have to let the phone ring 10 times before hanging up.
5. ___ It's better to take a shower in the morning than at night.

C Talk with a partner about your opinions.

1. What kinds of things do you like to discuss?
2. Do you have strong opinions about many things?
3. Do you think with your heart or your head?
4. Do you ever get angry when someone doesn't agree with you?

Level Up

When you are unsure of a source for some information you want to use in a debate or discussion, you can use the passive voice + "it."

Examples:
Some people say that illegal downloading is changing the music business.

▸ It has been said that illegal downloading is changing the music business.

Some sources report that very few people are buying CDs these days.

▸ It has been reported that very few people are buying CDs these days.

Rewrite these statements with a passive form of the verb + "it." Then compare your answers with a partner.

1. People claim that global warming is the most serious problem facing our planet.

_____

2. People say that tests don't really measure students' abilities.

_____

3. Some sources report that one can become fluent in a new language in just a year.

_____

4. People say that high school students don't have enough free time.

_____

5. Some sources report that many people eat all of their meals at fast-food restaurants.

_____

PROJECT 4

Future Plans

Evaluate how you have changed during this English course and what you plan to do in the future. Then present your ideas to your classmates.

A Discuss. These students have finished their English course. They are talking about their experiences and the future. How are you the same or different?

I've always been good at reading English, but speaking it was hard for me before this class. I've improved a lot, and to continue learning, I'm going to join an English conversation club.

I'd like to get a job for a multinational company after I graduate. The interviews are often in English, but I think this course has helped me prepare for them.

I never liked English before, but then I realized it was because I wasn't confident. By communicating actively, I've learned so much. Now, I'm going to sign up for more classes.

B Prepare. How have you changed, and what will you do next? Fill in the chart below.

Three ways I have changed since I started this course (e.g., English abilities, feelings about English, attitudes toward others or yourself).	1. _____ 2. _____ 3. _____
What I will do after this course, to: • keep or improve my skills. Or, •achieve some other goal related to English.	
My action plan to achieve my goal above:	

115

C **Create.** Make a poster to use in a presentation. Then practice the presentation.

How I have changed:

- I'm better at speaking English.

My action plan for the future:
- Join an English circle to improve my speaking skills even more.

I will:
- look into free English circles at City Hall.
- choose one and join.
- go to the circle at least once a week.

D **Present.** Explain how you have changed and what you intend to do in the future.

Example:
"I think this course has helped me become better at speaking English—and that was always hard for me in the past. However, I still need more practice speaking, so I plan to join an English circle . . ."

AUDIO SCRIPTS

1 Unit 1   Challenge Preview

Ana: Hi everyone, I'm Ana. I **designed** this emblem for Luis. When Luis was in high school, **soccer** was a big part of his life, so I drew a pair of soccer shoes. Luis used to play soccer on the high school team. They won the national championship.

Steven: Really? That's great.

Ana: Anyway, this book represents Luis' life now. He wants to improve his grades, so he is going to work harder this year. This picture of a book represents that.

Steven: Uh-huh.

Ana: This airplane represents the future. Luis said he'd like to travel around the world someday. He also wants to get a job in a foreign country.

2 Unit 1   Working on Fluency

1. Yumi: Well, Ana, it's a pretty exciting place . . .

Ana: Really?

Yumi: Yeah. There was always something to do.

Ana: Mm-hmm.

Yumi: And I really enjoyed growing up there.

Ana: I see. What did you like about it, Yumi?

Yumi: There were a lot of movie theaters, cafés, and really good clubs.

Ana: Hmm. That does sound fun.

2. Luis: Well, I had some good friends, but I guess I was pretty shy.

Ana: OK. How, for example?

Luis: Well, I didn't like to talk to other people in class.

Ana: I see. Are you still like that?

Luis: No, not at all.

Ana: Really?

Luis: Yeah, my friends say I'm the most talkative person they know.

3. Sang-mi: I don't know for sure, but I really like kids.

Ana: That's nice.

Sang-mi: Yeah, so maybe I can get a job teaching in a preschool or something.

Ana: Oh? Doing what?

Sang-mi: I think I'd like to be a teacher.

Ana: Hmm. Really?

Spoken English: Table of Contents

In this section, there are examples of important pronunciation features in American English.

1. Word Stress
2. Word and Sentence Stress
3. Syllables
4. Word and Sentence Stress
5. Linking Words
6. Linking Words with *t/d*
7. Intonation
8. Sentence Stress
9. Word Stress
10. Deletion
11. Pronunciation of the letter /s/
12. Intonation

Spoken English: Word Stress

A. Listen for the stressed syllable in these words on the audio CD.

deSIGNED
SOccer

B. Now practice these words:

1. emblem
2. national
3. improve
4. picture
5. travel
6. country

Unit 2   Challenge Preview

Yumi: My motto is "Friends first." I think it's important to be considerate and caring. My friends are important to me. **Let me explain.** Last year, I moved away from home and entered college.

Ethan: Uh-huh.

Yumi: There were so many new things in my life— a new school, new classmates— so I started to forget my old high school friends.

Ethan: Mm-hmm. **So what happened?**

Yumi: We stopped calling each other.

Then, when I went home during the vacation, I called my old friends but they were all "too busy" to meet me. I was really upset.

Ethan: Right. So what did you do?

Yumi: Well, I realized how important those old friends were. They were angry at me because I didn't stay in touch. So, I called them and apologized. Now, we're all friends again, and we keep in touch.

Unit 2   Working on Fluency

Woman: This is Glenda Liu from *Business Magazine*. Today, I'm interviewing the president of the online DVD rental company Instant Movie. Hello, Mr. Coleman. Please tell our viewers what your company does.

Man: Yes, we're a movie rental company. Members order DVDs from our website, and we mail them. After watching them, members mail them back to us. My company's slogan is "Simple, Speedy, Sure."

Woman: "Simple, Speedy, Sure." What does that mean?

Man: Well, it's simple because you can order DVDs from home, and it's speedy because you get the DVDs by express mail a day or so later.

Woman: OK, but, what do you mean by "sure"?

Man: What I mean is that you can be sure you'll get movies that you'll want to watch. We recommend movies we're sure you'll really like.

Woman: Do you mean you know what movies I like? How do you do that?

Man: Yes. We use a computer program that remembers the kinds of movies our customers rent. That way, we know what kind of movies they like.

Woman: Can you give me an example?

Man: Sure. Let's say you've rented an action movie starring a certain actor. When a new action movie with that star comes out, we'll recommend it.

Woman: Very interesting. Thank you for your time, Mr. Coleman.

Spoken English: Word and Sentence Stress

A. Listen for the most important word in these sentences on the audio CD. Then listen for the stressed syllable in those words.

> **Let me exPLAIN.**
> **So what HAPPened?**

B. Practice these sentences stressing the underlined words.
  1. I was <u>really</u> upset.
  2. So what did you <u>do</u>?
  3. <u>They</u> were angry at me.
  4. Thanks for <u>telling</u> me.

5 Unit 3 Challenge Preview

Sang-mi: Listen to this. I had a really embarrassing experience recently. I was taking the subway last month when this guy sat down next to me. As soon as he sat down, he said, "Hey, it's Kevin. How are you doing?"

Ethan: Did you know him?

Sang-mi: No, I didn't, but he was kind of cute, so I said, "I'm pretty good, thanks. How about you, Kevin?"

Ethan: And what did he say?

Sang-mi: Nothing—he didn't say anything, but after a while he asked, "What have you been doing recently?" Well, I thought that was a strange question, but I said, "Nothing much. How about you?"

Ethan: And?

Sang-mi: Well, he didn't answer, so I stood up and started to walk away. Just then, I heard him say "Let's have dinner." So, I turned to the guy and said, "Sorry. I don't think I know you." He just looked at me and said, "Do you mind? I'm on the phone."

6 Unit 3 Working on Fluency

Woman: Oh—who took my fruit?

Man: What's wrong?

Woman: I put my lunch and some fruit in the refrigerator this morning, and now the fruit is gone. Do you know anything about that?

Man: Um, no. I don't. Your fruit wasn't in the fridge when I looked.

Woman: Really?

Man: Um, yes. I made a cup of coffee when I came to work. I took some milk from the fridge, but I didn't see any fruit.

Woman: All right. Let me see. You told me that you made a cup of coffee.

Man: Uh-huh.

Woman: Where?

Man: In the kitchen.

Woman: OK. And you mentioned that you got milk from the fridge.

Man: That's right.

Woman: Mm-hmm. And you claimed that the fruit wasn't in the fridge. What else did you see?

Man: Hmm. Let me see. I saw somebody's lunch, I think.

Woman: Somebody's lunch, huh? Did you see any fruit?

Man: No. The apple was already gone.

Woman: Wait. You said that the apple was gone. How do you know it was an apple?

Man: Um. Oh dear. Um. Sorry. I didn't know it was your apple.

Spoken English: Syllables

A. Listen for the number of syllables in the <u>underlined</u> words on the audio CD. Then listen for the stressed syllables in those words.

I had a <u>RE-ALly</u> <u>emBARRassing</u>
　　　　　2 syllables　　4 syllables
<u>exPErience</u> recently.
　4 syllables

B. Now practice the sentences. Stress the CAPITALIZED syllables in the <u>underlined</u> words.

1. I had a pretty <u>FRIGHTening</u> <u>exPErience</u> the other day.
2. <u>SOMEthing</u> <u>VEry</u> <u>surPRIsing</u> <u>HAPpened</u> to me.
3. It was a <u>VEry</u> <u>FUNny</u> <u>situAtion</u>.
4. It was <u>absoLUTEly</u> <u>aMAZing</u>.

Luis:	What did you bring to class, Kirsten?
Kirsten:	This necklace.
Luis:	May I ask why it's special for you?
Kirsten:	My mom gave it to me when I graduated from high school.
Luis:	So you got it a few years ago, right?
Kirsten:	Yes, that's right. I've had it for three years.
Luis:	It's nice. Do you wear it often?
Kirsten:	Yeah, I've worn it every day since graduation.
Luis:	**It must be very special to you.**
Kirsten:	**Yes, it's very special.** If I have a daughter, I'll keep it until she graduates and then give it to her.

Yumi:	This book is really nice, Steven.
Steven	Thanks. I've had it a long time. It's about sports cars.
Yumi:	Sports cars . . . what kind of sports cars?
Steven	Um, Italian sports cars. I've been interested in them for a long time.
Yumi:	That's interesting. Why?
Steven	Oh, my uncle used to have an old Fiat.
Yumi:	An old Fiat. What was that like?
Steven	It was a red Fiat Spider from the 1970s. In fact, it was his first car. My uncle let me drive it once. Can you believe it? I actually drove a really cool Italian sports car.
Yumi:	That's nice. Well, when was that?
Steven	Let me think. It was about four years ago.
Yumi:	Four years ago. Anyway, tell me about your book.
Steven	Well, actually, there's a picture of my uncle's car in the book. Have a look.
Yumi:	Oh yeah . . . Hey, Steven, you said that you've had this book for a long time. How long?
Steven	A couple of years, I guess. Why?
Yumi:	Steven. It's a library book.
Steven:	A library book! Oh no!

Spoken English: Word and Sentence Stress

A. Listen for the most important word in these sentences on the audio CD. Then listen for the stressed syllables in those words.

> **It must be very SPEcial to you.**
> **Yes, it's VEry special.**

B. Now practice these sentences stressing the underlined words.

1. **A:** It must be really <u>VALuable</u>.
   B: Yes, it's <u>RE-ALly</u> valuable.
2. **A:** It must be pretty <u>imPORTant</u> to you.
   B: Yes, it's <u>PRETty</u> important.

Ana:	So, who would like to begin?
Ethan:	**I have an idea.** Let's make a class bulletin board.
Ana:	We could use it to display information.
Ethan:	OK, but what kind of information?
Ana:	You know, about school news, homework assignments, and other stuff.
Ethan:	Hmm. That sounds good.
Ana:	Yes, and **we could ask for advice and ideas** on how to study. As for me, I sometimes need help.
Ethan:	That's a really nice idea, Ana. Does anyone else have any suggestions?
Sang-mi:	You know, almost all of us have Internet access, so we could put the bulletin board on a class website instead.

10 Unit 5   Working on Fluency

Monica:	Hmm, so, how should we begin?
Daniel:	Well, first of all we need a group leader. How about you, Monica?
Monica:	Sure. I can do that.
Daniel:	I think we need someone to take notes too.
Monica:	How about you, Joe?
Joe:	Oh, OK. I'll do it. No problem.
Monica:	So, we need a plan. Joe—any ideas what we can do together?
Joe:	Actually, I'd like to have a party.
Monica:	OK. Well, what does everyone else think?
Hannah:	To tell you the truth, I'd rather do something that helps our studies.
Monica:	OK. Do you have any ideas how we can do that, Hannah?
Hannah:	Yeah. I'd like to start a study group. We could meet during lunchtime.
Joe:	That's an interesting idea, but I already study enough. I'd really like to do something fun.
Monica:	I understand that, but could we do something that's useful AND fun?
Daniel:	Well, we could plan an English-language lunch table. Each week one person thinks of a topic to discuss and brings something good to eat, like a dessert.

Spoken English: Linking Words

A. Listen to how words link together on the audio CD. Notice how the sound at the end of the first underlined word links to the sound at the beginning of the next underlined word.

> **I have an idea.**
> **We could ask for advice and ideas.**

B. Now practice these sentences. Link the first underlined word to the second in each.
1. That's a really nice idea.
2. Does anyone else have any suggestions?
3. People could access it from anywhere.
4. We could also put other stuff on the site.

🔘⑪ Unit 6 Challenge Preview

Steven: I love going out to eat, and Antonio's is one of my favorite places.

Yumi: OK, but **what do you like about it?**

Steven: Well, it has delicious Italian food and a really cozy atmosphere.

Yumi: That sounds good, but how are the prices? Is it expensive?

Steven: No, not really, so I go there all the time.

Yumi: Hmm. So where is it?

Steven: It's right across from the main station, so it's convenient too.

Yumi: Is it open late?

Steven: Yeah, it's open until 11 p.m. every day.

Yumi: I see. Can you go there just for dessert? I love tiramisu.

Steven: Yes, you can, and the portions are huge. One serving is enough for two people.

🔘⑫ Unit 6 Working on Fluency

Kirsten: Hey everybody. What's up?

Ethan: Hi, Kirsten.

Ana, Luis: Hi. Hey.

Kirsten: Do you guys know anything interesting happening this weekend?

Ethan: Why?

Kirsten: My cousin Amy is coming to visit. I've got to think of something to do with her.

Ana: How old is she?

Kirsten: 19, I think.

Ethan: And what's she interested in?

Kirsten: Typical stuff, I guess—shopping, restaurants, clubs—you know.

Luis: Well, why don't you take her sightseeing? How about the Sky Tower? You get a great view of the city from the top.

Kirsten: Hmm. Maybe.

Luis: Or, you could take her to the park next door. There's a music festival there this Saturday.

Kirsten: That sounds good. Thanks.

Ethan: You know, there's also an interesting exhibit at the art museum this weekend.

Kirsten: Um, I'm not sure. I don't think she likes art very much.

Ana: Then, how about eating out? Let me see. Café Deco is really nice.

Kirsten: That's not a bad idea.

Ana: And after dinner, you could take her to a club.

Kirsten: That's a really good idea. She really loves dancing . . .

Spoken English: Linking words with *t/d*

A. Listen to how words link together on the audio CD. Notice how the *t/d* sound is linked to the vowel sound at the beginning of the next word.

> Can you <u>recommend any</u> places near here to eat?
>
> What do you like <u>about it</u>?

B. Now practice these sentences.
1. Is it expensive?
2. It's right across from the main station.
3. Is it open late?
4. You mentioned that it's near here.
5. I'm kind of busy.

Ethan: **All you need to make this recipe is a sharp knife, a blender, and these ingredients: one lemon, sugar, ice, and four basil leaves.** And if you don't have any basil, you can use rosemary or a little Tabasco sauce.

Ethan: Anyway, here's what you do. First, peel the lemon and cut it into quarters.

Kirsten: Quarters—that means into four pieces?

Ethan: Exactly. Next, put the pieces of lemon in a blender along with some sugar. Add some ice cubes, a liter of water, and the basil. Then start the blender and mix it all at high speed for roughly 45 seconds.

Kirsten: Hey, that sounds easy.

Ethan: Yeah, it is. Finally, pour the lemonade into glasses, and serve.

🔘 14 **Unit 7**   **Working on Fluency**

Man: Welcome to "Sunday Kitchen." Today, Chef Marie Santos, star of the "Cooking with Marie" show from the Philippines, has joined us. Let's give her a big hand. So, what do you have for us today, Marie?

Woman: Well, today we're going to make a delicious chicken adobo. It's very popular in the Philippines—almost a national dish.

Man: Mmm.

Woman: OK. I have a chicken and all these ingredients for the adobo sauce: soy sauce, vinegar, garlic, a bay leaf, ginger, and black pepper.

Man: Hold on. Does it have to be a big chicken, like this one?

Woman: I don't know—how hungry are you? Anyway, cut a big chicken if you're hungry.

Man: Wait a second. Cut into how many pieces?

Woman: How many people are coming for dinner? You're funny. Anyway, now let's make the sauce. Put the other ingredients into a big bowl and mix them together with a spoon.

Man: OK. Then what?

Woman: Then put the chicken in the adobo and cook on very low heat until the chicken is done, then . . .

Man: Hang on. How long will that take?

Woman: Why? Are you hungry? It'll take about an hour, but here, try this. I made some before the show. It's served with rice.

Man: Oh, it's . . . delicious.

Spoken English: Intonation

A. Listen to the list of items on the audio CD. Notice how intonation rises and then drops at the end of the list.

All you need to make this recipe is a sharp knife, a blender, and these ingredients: one lemon, sugar, ice, and four basil leaves.

B. Now practice these lists.
1. Add some ice cubes, water, and basil.
2. Chop an onion, some carrots, and some celery into small pieces.
3. Mix the bananas with some lemon juice, honey, and melted butter.
4. Soy sauce, vinegar, garlic, a bay leaf, ginger, and black pepper.

15 Unit 8   Challenge Preview

Sang-mi:	Hello. **What kind of business is this?**
Luis:	Well, **it's an Asian restaurant** called East World.
Sang-mi:	Hmm. There are a lot of Asian restaurants around here. What's special about this one?
Luis:	Well, each table in the restaurant is shaped like a different country: Korea, Japan, China, and Thailand.
Sang-mi:	I see.
Luis:	You decide which cuisine you want to eat and sit at that table. For example, if you want to eat some Chinese food, sit at the Chinese table.
Sang-mi:	Right. And if you want a Korean meal, you sit at the table shaped like Korea.

16 Unit 8   Working on Fluency

Woman:	Welcome to "Business Report." I'm Christie Brown. Today, we're going to talk to the travel king Jonathan Lee, who's here to tell us about his chain of highly successful travel agencies—Easy Paradise . . . Mr. Lee, thanks for joining us.
Man:	My pleasure, Christie.
Woman:	So, Mr. Lee, how many branches of Easy Paradise are there now?
Man:	Let me see. We have more than 600 offices around the world now.
Woman:	Six hundred. Impressive. According to *Business World*, Easy Paradise is the fastest growing travel agency today. What makes it so successful?
Man:	I guess, Christie, it's because we guarantee the perfect holiday.
Woman:	What do you mean by "guarantee"?
Man:	I mean customers who have complaints about hotels or services get their money back.
Woman:	That's amazing. Have any customers done that?
Man:	Actually . . . a few have gotten their money back.
Woman:	And I suppose those people end up really happy about your service.
Man:	Exactly.
Woman:	I'm sure other companies will try to copy your business ideas, so what's next?
Man:	I can't give you too many details, but let's just say we're going to make an announcement very soon.
Woman:	Oh really? That sounds exciting. Mr. Lee, just a few more questions then . . .

Spoken English: Sentence Stress

A. Listen to the primary and secondary stress in these sentences on the audio CD.

What   kind of   <u>business</u> is   <u>this</u>?
                          (1)   (2)

It's an   <u>Asian</u>   <u>restaurant</u>.
              (1)   (2)

B. Now practice these sentences.

1. What's <u>special</u> about <u>this</u> one?
            (1)   (2)

2. You decide which <u>cuisine</u> you want to eat
                              (1)
   and sit at <u>that</u> table.
                  (2)

3. If you want to eat some <u>Chinese</u> food, sit
                                      (1)
   at the Chinese <u>table</u>.
                        (2)

124   Audio Scripts

17 Unit 9   Challenge Preview

Yumi: OK, Mr. Garcia, can you tell us a little bit about yourself?

Luis: Well, my friends say I'm a **pretty logical person**.

Steven: Logical?

Luis: Well, I like solving problems, and I'm good with numbers.

Ana: That's good. We're looking for **interior designers** to work in our office. They need to know how to use a computer. Do you have any computer experience, Mr. Garcia?

Luis: Absolutely. I took some computer classes in college, and I use a computer a lot at home.

Ana: That's great. Do you know how to use any computer-assisted design programs?

Luis: Well, I've used some of them, and I'm sure I can learn how to use any software you have. That's no problem.

18 Unit 9   Working on Fluency

Man: Thank you for coming in today, Ms. Lopez.

Ana: Oh, thank you for taking the time to talk with me.

Man: It's my pleasure. So how did you become interested in our company?

Ana: Well, I looked at your company website and some of the websites your company has designed. I was really impressed.

Man: Yes, we're very proud of our design work. I'm glad you like it. Now, I'd like to know more about you, Ms. Lopez. Tell me, what was college like for you?

Ana: It was good. I got As and Bs in all my classes, but I got all As in my computer classes.

Man: Computer classes?

Ana: That's right. My school offered several classes in computer programming. I took them all. I also took some digital photography classes.

Man: Great. A web designer should know something about photography— that's good. Did you take any classes on design as well?

Ana: Not really—I majored in English. However, I worked part-time in the English department's Multimedia Center.

Man: Multimedia Center? Could you tell me about that?

Ana: Of course. That's the computer center. I was the editor of our department's online newsletter. Last year, I gave it a new design.

Man: A new design? Please tell me more.

Ana: Well, first of all, I . . .

Spoken English: Word Stress

A. Listen to the stress patterns in these phrases on the audio CD.

> PREtty LOgical PERson
> inTERior designers

B. Now practice these words.
1. computer experience
2. computer classes
3. computer-assisted design programs
4. good people skills

Kirsten:	Will Jessica be able to answer the professor's tough questions and win $1 million? Let's watch.
Steven:	OK, Jessica. Here's the first question. What's the longest word in the English language?
Jessica:	Let me see. I don't know. The longest word. Oh dear.
Steven:	Come on. You can do it, Jessica. Think about it. What's the longest word?
Jessica:	I give up! I'm really sorry but I just don't know.
Steven:	Don't give up, Jessica. Give me a big smile. Jessica, that's a hint.
Jessica:	I've got it! The longest word in the English language is "smiles."
Steven:	That's right! Congratulations! Now, for $10,000, can you tell us why?
Jessica:	I sure can! The longest word is "smiles" because there's a "mile" between the first and last letters.
Steven:	That's right. Congratulations!

Steven:	Hey Sang-mi, what do you think is on TV tonight? Hand me the remote control.
Sang-mi:	OK. Here you are.
Man 1:	Tonight at 6, another great episode of "Crazy Kid," the funniest sitcom of the year. Watch how Jenny gets in trouble with Mom over her grades.
Mom:	Do you have something for me? Your report card?
Daughter:	Yes, I have it. It's right here.
Mom:	Well, are you going to give it to me?
Daughter:	Yes, but wait. I have to know one thing first. What are you going to do to me after I give it to you?
Steven:	Yuck. What else is on?
Man 2:	*Spy Attack*, the action film of the year.
Woman 1:	Do you have something for me, Jack? The gun?
Man 3:	Yes, I have it. It's right here.
Woman 1:	Well, are you going to give it to me?
Man 3:	Yes, but wait. I have to know one thing first. What are you going to do to me after I give it to you?
Man 2:	*Spy Attack*. In theaters now.
Sang-mi:	Hmm.
Man 1:	Don't miss "The Lovers" tonight at 9, when Josh asks Mandy to marry him.
Woman 2:	Do you have something for me? Maybe a diamond ring?
Man 2:	Yes, I have it. It's right here.
Woman 2:	So are you going to give it to me?
Man 2:	Yes, but wait. I have to know one thing first. What are you going to do to me after I give it to you?
Sang-mi:	You know, lately, it seems every show is the same.

Spoken English: Deletion

A. Listen to how words link together on the audio CD. Notice how a final /t/ sound in the <u>underlined</u> word is dropped when the following word begins with a consonant sound.

   A̶t̶ 7 p.m.
   Don'̶t̶ miss the exciting new episode.

B. Now practice these sentences.
   1. Here's the <u>first</u> question.
   2. <u>Let</u> me see.
   3. I <u>don't</u> know.
   4. Think <u>about</u> it.

21

Unit 11 Challenge Preview

Sang-mi: Hi Yumi. What's your dilemma?

Yumi: OK, um, this story isn't about me—it's about my cousin. Fumi has fallen in love with someone she met online, and **she says she's really in love with this guy.** They chat a lot online, and they've met each other a few times. The guy seems really nice, and now they're talking about getting married.

Sang-mi: **So . . . what's the problem, then?**

Yumi: Well, the problem is Fumi's parents. They are kind of old-fashioned, and they don't like the situation at all. They've ordered Fumi to stop talking to the guy and find a "real" boyfriend. So, here's my question: What would you do if you were Fumi?

Sang-mi: Hmm. Well, if I were Fumi, I'd probably talk to my parents and try to make them understand.

22

Unit 11 Working on Fluency

Roy: Welcome back, this is "All Talk Radio." I'm Roy.

Jamie: And I'm Jamie. What's in the news today?

Roy: Well, you won't believe this, but a 14-year-old girl has sued her brother for eating her ice cream cone.

Jamie: You're kidding. She sued her own brother? For eating her ice cream?

Roy: Yep, she hired a lawyer and took him to court.

Jamie: Well, personally, I believe that's just wrong. It's too much.

Roy: Just between you and me, I agree. But the thing is . . . she won!

Jamie: So, what's the story?

Roy: Let me see. The girl offered her brother a bite of her ice cream cone, but he ate the whole thing. Then she sued him. So let's hear what some of our listeners have to say.

Jamie: The whole thing! Hmm, that's pretty mean.

Roy: Yeah, but let's hear what some of our listeners have to say. You're on the air. Who's this, and what do you think?

Mark: Hi, I'm Mark. To be honest, I think the whole thing is silly. It's just ice cream, right? Why didn't the girl just buy another cone?

Roy: Maybe she didn't have enough money. Who knows? Anyway, thanks.

Jamie: Who's next? You're on the air.

Lindie: I'm Lindie. You know, I think the girl has a point.

Jamie: Really? How so?

Lindie: In my opinion, that girl's brother needs to be taught a lesson.

Jamie: But to sue him . . . in a court of law?

Lindie: I guess that's a little too much, but her brother acted like a bully. I shouldn't say this, but that kind of thing can lead to bigger problems, even crime!

Jamie: You're right! Maybe you shouldn't say that! But you did! Thanks. And we'll be back right after this commercial break . . . then tell us what you think.

Spoken English: Pronunciation of the letter /s/

A. Listen to how the final /s/ sound is pronounced with both a /z/ and and /s/ sound on the audio CD.

   She <u>says</u> she's really in love with this guy.

   So, <u>what's</u> the problem, then?

B. Now practice these sentences.

   1. <u>What's</u> your dilemma?

   2. So, <u>here's</u> my question:

   3. The problem is <u>Fumi's</u> parents.

23 Unit 12 Challenge Preview

Ethan: These days, downloading music off the Internet without paying for it has become really common.

Kirsten: Let's look at the first point. It's stealing. I heard that somebody went to jail for downloading music without paying for it. I don't want to go to jail for downloading music illegally. Do you?

Ethan: Now let's talk about how illegal downloading hurts musicians. Nobody makes music for free. It's a job. **For example, when somebody records a song, he or she should be paid for it.**

Kirsten: Seriously, everybody should support their favorite bands by buying music—not by stealing it! If everybody downloaded music illegally, bands wouldn't get any money. Without money, nobody would make new CDs. Do you want that to happen?

24 Unit 12 Working on Fluency

Ethan: . . . For these reasons, we strongly believe that people should stop downloading music illegally.

Steven: OK. First of all, you said that somebody went to jail for downloading music illegally. Huh? This simply isn't true. According to an article I read recently, nobody has gone to jail for downloading music. However, some free music sites have been shut down.

Ana: That's right. Then you claimed that musicians just want money. Maybe big stars, but lots of bands, especially indie bands, make music because they love music.

Steven: Exactly. For instance, one of my favorite new bands gives away their music for free on the Internet. They just want people to hear it.

Ana: Yeah. And here's something to think about. In my experience, people who download a band's songs are more likely to buy the band's CDs later.

Steven: That's for sure! For example, a friend of mine recommended a band recently, so I downloaded some of their music. I loved it, so I bought all their CDs and saw them live. They were awesome!

Ana: Finally, you said that downloading music is dangerous because of computer viruses. Everyone knows it's not that dangerous. Let me tell you why. Lots of people download music these days, but you hardly ever hear about someone getting a virus from it. Besides, . . .

Spoken English: Intonation

A. Listen to the audio CD. Notice the falling intonation before the comma (,).

> **For example, when somebody records a song, he or she should be paid for it.**

B. Now practice these sentences.
1. If everybody downloaded music illegally, bands wouldn't get any money.
2. Last year, my computer got a virus.